THE SUTRA
OF THE SIXTH PATRIARCH
ON THE
PRISTINE ORTHODOX DHARMA

六祖法寶壇禪經

THE SUTRA
OF THE SIXTH PATRIARCH
ON THE
PRISTINE ORTHODOX DHARMA

AN ORIGINAL PUBLICATION OF THE
BUDDHA'S UNIVERSAL CHURCH
720 WASHINGTON STREET
SAN FRANCISCO, CALIFORNIA

TRANSLATED FROM THE CHINESE BY

PAUL F. FUNG, M.A., M.D., PH.D.
GEORGE D. FUNG, M.A., M.D., PH.D.

For information address:

BUDDHA'S UNIVERSAL CHURCH
720 Washington Street
San Francisco, California 94108
(415) 982-6116

Printed in the United States of America

CONTENTS

PREFACE

This sutra, or scripture, is considered to be one of the greatest in Buddhist literature. It was spoken by the Six Patriarch, Hui Neng, in China almost 1300 years ago. He was the last of the officially designated patriarchs in direct lineage from the days of the Buddha. This sutra is, and has long been, widely revered in China and Japan, because of its concise and powerful expressions of the doctrines of Mahayana Buddhism.

This scripture has been chosen by the Research Council of the Buddha's Universal Church as its first translation from the Chinese into modern, easily understandable English. Incidentally, this church is the largest hand-built Buddhist church in America. Its construction by the members and volunteers spanned eleven years and four months.

Much of the highly interesting discussion in the footnotes and glossary that adds so much to the meaning of the sutra itself, is from original material in the Chinese which, heretofore, has never been translated into English.

The entire translation has taken more than ten years during which it has undergone numerous revisions in an attempt to bring out in the English language the full power, unique flavor, and great significance which the sutra has in the original Chinese.

It may be of interest to note that two lines in the scripture have been posted in the Buddha's Universal Church, through all the years of its construction.

"It is a fundamental principle of Buddhism not to argue.
To argue is to lose the meaning of the way."

San Francisco

Paul F. Fung, M.A., M.D., Ph.D.
George D. Fung, M.A., M.D., Ph.D.

CHAPTER I

MY TRAVELS

行由品

On the occasion of the arrival of the Great Master[1] at Pao Lin[2] (monastery), the Prefect Wei Chu of Shao Chou[3] and his officials went to the mountain to invite the Master to come down to the lecture hall of the Ta Fan Temple[4] in the heart of the city, so that an opportunity will be open to all to hear him speak about the Dharma.[5]

When the Master went up to the throne, there were assembled the Prefect, some thirty officials, more than thirty Confucian scholars, and over one thousand monks, nuns, Taoists, and laymen.

They all paid their respects, expressing their desire to hear the essentials of the Dharma. The Great Master addressed the gathering, saying:

"Virtuous and learned counselors,[6] the wisdom,[7] of our self-nature[8] is at root clear and quiet. You have but to use this mind to directly become a Buddha.[9]

"Virtuous and learned counselors, listen now to what transpired up to my realization of the Dharma. My father was a native of Fan Yang.[10] He was officially discharged (from his position) and banished to Ling Nan[11] to be a commoner in Hsin Chou.[12] My start in life was inauspicious, for my father died early leaving my old mother destitute. We moved to Nan Hai[13] (where we lived) in hardship and poverty by selling kindling in the market place.

"On one occasion a customer, buying kindling, ordered me to deliver it to his shop. When he had received delivery and I had been paid, I came out of the door and heard a man reciting a sutra.[14] As I listened to the words of the sutra, my mind was at once opened to direct awakening.

"Thereupon, I asked the man what sutra he was reciting. He replied, 'The Diamond Sutra.'[15] I asked him further from where he had come and why he observed this sutra. He replied, 'I am from the Eastern Ch'an Temple,[16] in Ch'i Chou,[17] in the District of Huang Mei.[18] This is the temple of the Fifth Patriarch Hung Jen,[19] where he is the teacher of more than a thousand disciples. When I went there to pay him my respects and to listen (to his instructions), I received this sutra. The Great Master regularly teaches both monks and laymen that if only they will observe the Diamond Sutra, they will be able to see into their self-nature and can directly become Buddhas.'

"As I listened to these words, (I realized that I must have) had a past affinity for them. Whereupon a customer made me a gift of ten taels,[20] advising me to provide adequate food and clothing for my old mother, and then to set out for Huang Mei to pay my respects to the Fifth Patriarch and to study the doctrine under him.

"When I had finished all that was necessary for the care of my mother, I took leave at once. In less than thirty days I arrived in Huang Mei. As I paid my respects to the Fifth Patriarch, he asked, 'What district do you come from? What do you seek?'

"I am a Buddhist pupil from Ling Nan and of the common people of Hsin Chou. I have come from a great distance to make my respects to you and to seek to become a Buddha, O Master, and for no other reason.

"The Patriarch replied, 'You are a native of Ling Nan and just a boor. How can you possibly become a Buddha!'

"I answered, 'There are of necessity southern and northern people, but from the standpoint of the Buddha-nature, there is at root neither South nor North. The appearance of a boor is not the same as a monk, but what difference does this make in terms of Buddha-nature?'

"The Fifth Patriarch wished to continue the conversation, but as he saw that many of his disciples were now gathering around, he ordered me to join the group and to go to work.

"But I said, 'Venerable Sir, may I tell you that discriminating-alertness [21] arises continuously in my own mind, and that in not straying from one's self-nature one is (already cultivating) the field-of-merits. [22] I have not yet asked you, Venerable Sir, what work you would have me do.'

"The Patriarch replied, 'You are a boor, yet a great wit. You may stop talking.'

"He ordered me off to the granary. I then withdrew to the back court where there was an attendant who told me to chop wood and to pound rice.

"After a little more than eight months, the Patriarch happened to see me one day and said, 'I feel that your

3

understanding is acceptable, but I fear there may be people of ill will who might harm you. Thus I have not spoken with you. Do you understand me?'

"I replied, 'I know what you mean, Master, and that is why I have not ventured up to the hall, lest others might notice me.'

"On one occasion the Master summoned his disciples together. When they were all assembled he said, 'I have something to tell you. Man's birth and death is a serious matter. The whole crowd of you, from one day's end to another, are seeking only the field-of-merits. You are not seeking deliverance from the bitter ocean of births and deaths.

'If you are deluded in your self-nature, how can wealth save you? Everyone of you go and look within yourself for the knowledge of discriminating-alertness. Realize the nature of prajna[23] (wisdom) from your own original mind. Everyone of you compose a poem. Bring it to me to see. If you have awakened to the fundamental essence (of the teachings), I will bequeath you the robe and the Dharma, and you will become the Sixth Patriarch. Go like wild fire! Do not dally! Mulling over it is useless! A person who realizes his own nature, realizes it as soon as it is mentioned. If you are such an individual, even amidst the whirling swords of battle you will still realize it.'

"Having received this order everyone withdrew. But discussing it among themselves, they said, 'It is not necessary for all of us to calm our minds and to concentrate on composing a poem to give to the Patriarch. What good will it do? Shen Hsiu[24] is the head monk and is now our instructor. He will certainly get it (i.e. the patriarchate).

4

It would be a farce and a waste of mental energy for us to write poems for recitation.' All of them heard this discussion (and accordingly) were satisfied.

"They all said among themselves, 'Thereafter, we shall follow Hsiu as our master. So why bother to compose poems?'

"Shen Hsiu reflected, 'They are not going to present any poem because I am their instructor. Therefore I must compose a poem and present it to the Patriarch. If I do not offer a poem, how will the Patriarch know whether the realization of my mind is deep or shallow? In presenting the poem, if my intention is just to seek the Dharma, it will be virtuous. But if I am (simply) looking for the patriarchate, it will be evil. My attitude would be identical with that of the common man if I sought to deprive him of his office. How am I to decide? If I do not offer a poem, I shall never get the Dharma. What a predicament! What a quandary!'

"In the front part of the Fifth Patriarch's hall, there were three corridors, where it had been decided to invite the devout and worshipful Lu Chen [25] to paint the transformation scenes from the Lankavatara Sutra [26] and also the chart of the lineage up to the Fifth Patriarch, so that it might be venerated by future generations.

"When Shen Hsiu had composed a poem, he sought to present it several times. But when he reached the front of the hall, a turmoil of anxiety arose in his mind and his whole body dripped with perspiration. He could not make up his mind to submit it. In four days he went back and forth thirteen times, yet could not bring himself to offer the poem.

5

"Hsiu then pondered, 'Why not write it on the wall of the corridor? When the Patriarch chances upon it and should he speak well of it, then I will go forth and make obeisance, saying that I composed it! But if he says it is not suitable, I would have wasted several years in this mountain receiving the people's homage. Then what is the use of continuing on?'

"That night during the third watch,[27] while holding a lamp and without letting anyone know, he wrote on the wall of the southern corridor the poem which represented his realization. The poem read:

> The body is a Bodhi[28] tree,
> The mind, a bright mirrored stand.
> Whisk it continuously and zealously,
> Allowing no dust to cling.

"Hsiu finished writing the poem and returned at once to his room without anyone knowing about it. Again he ruminated, 'Tomorrow the Fifth Patriarch will see the poem, and if he is glad, then I have an affinity with the Dharma. But if it is not acceptable then I am still in delusion because of the heavy hindrances of my past, and it will not be fitting for me to receive the Dharma. The Master's mind is difficult to fathom.'

"In his own room as he pondered, he would sit and then (sometimes) would lay down. He was unable to rest until the fifth watch (at daybreak).

"The Patriarch already knew that Shen Hsiu was not able to enter the gate[29] because he had not realized his self-nature. At daybreak the Patriarch summoned Lu, the visiting housemanager, (and went with him) to the South corridor wall where the paintings of the chart and figures were to be done. Suddenly, they saw this poem. Turning (to the manager) the Patriarch said, 'It really is not necessary to do the paintings. I regret that you should have come so far. For as the sutra says, 'All that has form is empty and vain.'[30] But leave this poem for the people to study and recite. Practice in accordance with this poem prevents one from falling into evil paths: practice in accordance with this poem brings great benefits. Let the disciples light incense and pay reverence, that they may observe this poem fully. They will then be able to realize their true nature.'

"The disciples all observed the poem and exclaimed, 'Indeed, it is wonderful!'

"But at the third watch the Patriarch summoned Hsiu to his quarters and asked him, 'Did you compose this poem or not?'

"Hsiu replied, 'Yes, I composed it. I dare not presume to seek the patriarchate but I hope, Venerable Sir, that in your compassion, you will see whether or not this student has a little prajna.'

"The Patriarch answered, 'In writing this poem (you show that) you have not yet realized your original nature. You have only approached the door (of the Dharma); you have not yet entered it. The boundless awakening, [31] sought with your present views, is definitely unattainable.

'Boundless awakening means that even in the most minute verbalization, you know your own mind. You realize your own nature, that it does not start (any thoughts), so there are none to be stopped. At all times you realize your own self from one moment's thought to another. The

7

ten thousand things (are not discriminated and so) do not stagnate. The one reality without magnification or mini-mization is the same reality for all. Then ten thousand situations (will be seen to be) just as they are. The mind's suchness-of-things-just-as-they-are, is the real gem of realization. If you realize it in this way, then this is in-deed the boundless awakening of one's self-nature!

'Now go away for one or two days. Think about what I have said. Write another poem and bring it to me to see. Should your poem (show that you) are able to enter the gate, I will bestow upon you the robe and the Dharma!'

"Paying his respects, Shen Hsiu retired. Again sev-eral days passed, he (tried but) was unable to compose another poem. His mind was agitated and his spirit rest-less. He went about like one in a dream---dejected.

"Two days later it happened that a boy passed the rice-milling room chanting the poem. Upon hearing it, Hui Neng knew at once that (the writer of) this poem had not yet realized his original nature. For, although he had not yet received any instructions, he was already aware of the fundamental principles. Whereupon he asked the boy, 'What is that poem you are reciting?'

"The boy replied, 'Of course, a rustic like you would-n't know! But the Great Master has said that man's birth and death is a momentous event and that he wants to be able to pass on the robe and the Dharma. (Therefore) he has ordered his disciples to compose and submit a poem. If (there is one) who has realized the fundamental princi-ple, that one will receive the robe and the Dharma, and will become the Sixth Patriarch.

'Shen Hsiu, the head monk (sthavira), has written this

8

poem of the formless on the wall of the South corridor. The Great Master has allowed all his disciples to recite it and to put it into practice so that they may not fall into evil ways. The practice of this poem confers great benefits.'

"Hui Neng said, 'O Wise One, I have been treading the pestle here for more than eight months and I have not yet been up to the hall. I hope that you, O Wise One, will lead me to this poem, so that I may pay my respects to it.'

"The boy led him to where the poem was written, so that he might pay his respects. Hui Neng said, 'I cannot read characters, O Wise One. Will you please read them for me?'

"At that moment, there was present an official of the Chiang Chou [32] province named Chang Jih Yung, (張日用) who started to read the poem in a loud voice. After Hui Neng had listened, he said, 'I also have a poem, and I hope this official will write it for me.'

"The official said, 'You also have composed a poem! This is very extraordinary!'

"Turning to the official, Hui Neng said, 'If you wish to attain the boundless awakening, sir, you must not slight a beginner. A person of the lowest class may have a super-ior understanding, whereas a person of the highest class may have only the dead idea of understanding.'

"The official replied, 'You just recite your poem, and I will write it for you. If you should receive the Dharma, you must deliver me first. Do not forget this request.'

9

"My poem was:

The very essence of Bodhi has no tree,
Nor is there a bright mirrored stand.
In reality there is nothing,
So what is there to attract any dust.

"When this poem had been written, all the disciples crowded around in excitement. There was not one who did not express admiration. They all said among themselves, 'This is most extraordinary. (It shows) one can't judge a person by his outward appearance. How is it for so long we had not recognized a Bodhisattva[33] in the flesh.'

"When the Patriarch saw the astonishment of the excited crowd, he was afraid that there might be those (who would do me) harm. He rubbed off the poem with his slipper, saying, 'This one also has not yet realized his own nature,' and everyone took it to be so.

"The next day, the Patriarch went silently to the milling room. He saw me pounding rice by shoving my body against a kidney-shaped stone. He asked, 'Should one who seeks the Dharma be like this?' and then went on, 'Is the rice done yet?'

"I replied, 'The rice has been done for sometime. It still needs to be sifted.'[34] With his staff, the Patriarch struck the stone-mill three times, then left. I immediately understood the Patriarch's meaning; at the third watch I went to his room. Using his robe as a screen, so that no one should see, the Patriarch instructed me in the Diamond Sutra up to the passage, 'Should there be nothing to which one is attached (in this physical world), then the mind is in its (right) abode!'[35] Upon hearing this statement I immediately had the great awakening...that the ten thousand

10

things were not separate from my self-nature!

"Thereupon, I addressed the Patriarch, saying, 'Who would have known that one's self-nature is of itself fundamentally clear and pure. Who would have known that one's self-nature does not give rise to anything and so nothing has to be terminated! Who would have known that one's self-nature is of itself basically perfect! Who would have known that one's self-nature is originally without agitation! Who would have known that one's self-nature can give rise to the ten thousand things!'

"The Patriarch, knowing that I had the awakening to the original nature, spoke to me, saying, 'If you do not know the original mind, studying the Dharma is useless. If you know your original mind, you will realize your own original nature. You will then be called a man of spirit, a teacher of devas and men, a Buddha.'

"In the third watch I received the Dharma without any other person knowing about it. Thereupon, he also bequeathed to me the Sudden School, the robe, and the bowl, saying, 'You are to become the Sixth Patriarch. Take good care of yourself. On all sides deliver those who have the disposition. Spread (the Dharma) for future generations. Do not allow it to come to an end. Listen to my poem:

Where there is the disposition, plant the seed;
According to its grounds (i.e. affinities), the
    fruits will grow.
Where there is no affinity, no seed will hold;
Where the nature is barren, nothing will grow.

"The Patriarch continued, 'Many years ago, the great

master, Bodhidharma[36] first came to this land. People in general did notyet have any knowledge or confidence (in this teaching). Therefore, he bequeathed this robe as a symbol of the faith, and it was thus accepted from generation to generation. But the Dharma is transmitted from one mind to another, which is the way of self-awakening and self-realization. Since ancient times, the fundamental principles have been transmitted from Buddha to Buddha, and the original Dharma have been passed on secretly from master to master. Since the robe may become a cause of contention, its transmission must cease with you. If you pass on the robe, your life will hang by a thread. You should leave quickly. I fear there are those who may harm you.'

"Where," I asked, "shall I go?"

"The Patriarch replied, 'Stay in Huai[37] and hide in Hui.'[38]

"At the third watch, I received the robe and the bowl. The Fifth Patriarch accompanied me to the Chiu-chiang[39] posthouse and into a boat. Thereupon, I immediately took hold of the oar, but the Patriarch said, 'It is appropriate that I should be rowing you.'

"But I replied, 'When in delusion, the Master is the guide. When awakened, one guides oneself. To guide (and to be guided) is the same word, yet the applications are different according to the understanding. However, I was born in the frontier country and my pronunciation may be incorrect. But since you have graciously given me the Dharma, and having now attained awakening, it is only proper that I should guide myself by my own nature.'

"The Patriarch replied, 'So it is. So it is. From now on the breadth of the spread of Buddhism will depend upon you. You had better travel vigorously to the South. There is no need to be loquacious, for it is difficult to understand the more profound principles of Buddhism!'

"When I had respectfully taken leave of the Patriarch, I began to walk to the South. In about two months I reached the Ta Yu Mountains [40] (in Kiangsi).

"When the Fifth Patriarch returned, he did not appear in the hall for several days. The community began to be anxious and to inquire after his health asking, 'Venerable Sir, aren't you feeling quite well?'

"He replied, 'There is no sickness. The robe and the Dharma have already gone to the South.' 'To whom,' they asked, 'did you bequeath it?' and he answered, 'He who is capable has received it.' It was thus that the community found out what had happened.

"Whereupon several hundred persons set out in pursuit of the robe and bowl, (and among them) was a monk named Ch'en Hui Ming [41] who was formerly a general of the fourth class, a man of very rough character. He was so intent upon the pursuit that he was the first person of the group to catch up with me. I tossed the robe and the bowl upon the top of a rock; for since this represented the faith, could one achieve it with violence? Then I hid myself among the tall grasses. When Hui Ming came to pick up the robe and bowl to take them away, he could not move them. Whereupon he called out saying, 'Lay Brother, Lay Brother, I came for the Dharma; I did not come for the robe.'

"So I came out and sat on top of the rock with my

legs crossed. Hui Ming bowed to me saying, 'Lay Brother, may I hope that you will instruct me in the Dharma?'

"I replied, 'Since you have come for the Dharma, you should be able to calm all the incidents (in your mind). Do not evoke a single thought and I will instruct you.'

"It took Ming quite a while (to do it). Then I said, 'When you are not thinking good and not thinking evil, at that very moment, would that be the Venerable Hui Ming's original appearance?'[42] At these words Hui Ming had the great awakening.

"But he asked further saying, 'In addition to these secret instructions and meanings which you have received from the Fifth Patriarch, is there still any further secret meaning?'

"I answered, 'According to your question, you have not attained the secret meaning. If you will but reflect within yourself, you will find that the secret is right next to you.'

"Hui Ming then said, 'Even though I had been at Huang Mei, I never actually awakened to my (original) appearance. Now that I have received your direct instructions, it is just like a person drinking water and knowing for himself whether it is cold or warm. And now, Dharma Brother, you are my master.'

"I replied, 'If this is the way you feel, then the master of both of us is the one at Huang Mei. Cherish carefully what you have learned.'

"Hui Ming asked again, 'Hereafter how shall I go.'

"When you are confused by an incident you should stop," I answered, "and when you have the virtuous understanding you may continue to think.

"Ming respectfully departed. Thereafter, he changed his name to Tao Ming to avoid having the same first name as his Master's.

"Afterwards I came to Ts'ao Ch'i [43] but was again harassed and pursued by ill-disposed people. So I stayed out of trouble by lodging at Szu Hui [44] with a group of hunters. In that neighborhood I expounded the sutras for fifteen years. According to the propriety of the occasions, I also spoke about the Dharma to the hunters.

"The hunters always used to order me to watch their traps, but whenever I saw a living creature, I released it if it were possible. At meal times, they cooked meat in the same pot with the vegetables. If I was asked (to share), I replied, 'I will just pick the vegetables out of the meat.'

"One day I began to think seriously that it was the proper time to spread the Dharma, rather than to keep it concealed all the time. So I went to the Fa Hsing Monastery [45] at Kwang Chou, [46] where at that time the Dharma Master Yin Tsung was expounding the Nirvana Sutra. [47] (At this monastery) two monks happened to be discussing the wind and flag problem. One was maintaining that the wind moves, the other was maintaining that the flag moves. They were discussing it back and forth without coming to any conclusion. I came forward and said, 'Neither the wind nor the flag is moving, kind sirs, it is the mind that moves.'

"The whole group was astonished at this. Thereupon

15

Yin Tsung invited me to one of the upper seats and inter-
rogated me about the subtle points (of the doctrine). He
saw that while my words were simple, I had a direct grasp
of the principle which was not from book-learning.

"Tsung said, 'Good sir, you are definitely not an ordinary person. A long time ago, I heard from Huang Mei
that the robe and the Dharma had come to the South.
Might you be that one, kind sir?'

"I replied, 'Indeed, I am that unworthy one.'

"Yin Tsung thereupon bowed to me, and publicly invited me to bring out the robe and bowl to show them to
the entire community. He further asked me, saying, 'What
kind of teaching was given at Huang Mei?'

"I replied, 'There was no special teaching given. We
were told only to look into our own nature. There was no
discussion of meditation and liberation.'

"Tsung asked, 'Why was there no discussion of meditation and liberation?'

"I answered him, 'Because that is a dualistic doctrine.
That is not Buddhism. Buddhism is not a dualistic doctrine.'

"Tsung asked again, 'In what way is Buddhism not a
dualistic doctrine?'

"I answered, 'If you are a Dharma Master who ex-
pounds the Nirvana Sutra, and realizes his Buddha-nature,
you would certainly understand that Buddhism is not a
dualistic doctrine.'

"For instance, as Raja Kao Kuei Te,[48] a Boddhisattva,

16

once asked the Buddha, 'If one should violate the four inhibitions[49] and commit the five misdeeds,[50] or is a heretic (icchantika), would it break off the good root of Buddha-nature?'

"The Buddha answered, 'Virtuous roots are of two varieties, one that is permanent and the other that is impermanent. But the Buddha-nature[51] is not permanent, yet it is not impermanent. It cannot be divided. Therefore, it is called non-dualistic. One is virtuous, the other is not virtuous. But the Buddha-nature is not virtuous, yet it is not non-virtuous. Therefore, it is called non-dualistic. An ordinary man sees the world of the five skandhas[52] with its dualism, but the man of wisdom knows there is no such dualism. Such non-dualistic nature is identical with the Buddha-nature.

"Hearing this Yin Tsung joyfully put his palms together in the position of respect and said, 'When others expound the sutra, it is like the rumbling of the tiles, but your discussion, good sir, is like pure gold.'

"Thereupon he gave me the tonsure and also wanted me to be his Master. I then opened the Tung Shan School[53] beneath the Bodhi tree (that stood there), for I had received the Dharma at Tung Shan. I had had my fill of hardships and (there were times when) my life had hung by a thread.

"To be able to be with you today, my lord prefect, court officials, monks, nuns, Taoists, and laymen, altogether in one gathering, must be the coincidental interrelationships of the good causations in our collective pasts. It must also be because we have made devout offerings to the various Buddhas during many past lives, that we have together grown roots of good merits making it possible for us to hear this Sudden Doctrine and receive the Dharma。

"The teaching has been transmitted from previous Patriarchs. It is not of my own wisdom。 If you want to hear the teaching of the old Patriarchs you must all let your minds become clear。 After you have heard it, you should cast away from yourselves all hesitation and doubt and then you will be no different from those sages of ancient times."

FOOTNOTES

1   The Great Master is the Sixth Patriarch, Hui Neng, 慧能 , of China, 638 A.D. to 713 A.D.

2   Pao Lin 寶林
Pao Lin Monastery, 寶林寺 , also known as Ts'ao Ch'i Nan Hua Monastery, 曹溪南華寺 , at Nan Hai, 南海 , originally built in 505 A.D., 梁天監三年 . This is the monastery where the Sixth Patriarch spoke the sutra that bears his name. Sixty li south of Shao Chou, 韶州 .

3   Shao Chou 韶州
A district formerly of Ch'u Chiang, 曲江 , now a part of Kwang-tung, 廣東 .

4   Ta Fan Temple 大梵寺 .
The Ta Fan Temple is in the district of Shao Chou. It was first rebuilt in 715 A.D., 唐開元二年 .

5   Dharma 法
When Dharma is used as the law or the doctrine, or the principles of Buddhism, then the capital will be used. When it is used as one of the elements or things e.g., 萬法 , the ten thousand things or elements, the small d will be used.

6   Virtuous and learned counselors 善知識
Chapter XXV of the Nirvana Sutra, 涅槃經二十五 , defines virtuous and learned counselors, 善知識 , as those who are capable of teaching (the Dharma), 能教眾生 , far-removed from the ten evils, 遠離十惡 , and have practiced the ten virtues, 修行十善 . This term of address to the Sixth Patriarch's audience implies that they are not beginners in the study or practice of Buddhism. This term is frequently used by the Sixth Patriarch because his sutra was intended for the more advanced disciples.

7   Wisdom, bodhi 菩提
Bodhi (from the sanskrit, budh) means knowledge, understanding and perfect wisdom. It is also the name of the tree under which the Buddha attained his final enlightenment, the Bodhi tree.

8   Self-nature, 自性 , svabhana.
In the Chinese, 自 , is self, own, one's own; and 性 , nature, spirit, soul---so that self-nature is one's innate or spiritual nature,

or one's natural nature. The use of natural is in the pristine sense of the original state. To arrive at this natural state by the freeing of all bonds of attachments and defilements is one of the important points of the sutra.

9   Buddha 佛
A person who has completely freed himself from all attachments, attained the perfect wisdom and ultimate enlightenment. The Buddha is not God, but is recognized as a great teacher of the eternal truths.

10   Fan Yang 范陽
An ancient region in Hopei, 河北 , Province composed of several counties.

11   Ling Nan, 嶺南 ; 嶺 , mountains; 南 , south.
'South of the mountains' in the area that is now part of Kwangtung.

12   Hsin Chou 新州
A district in Kwangtung Province south of the mountains, now known as Hsin Shing, 新興 , County.

13   Nan Hai 南海
The name of a district in Kwangtung.

14   Sutra 經
Scriptures, but more restrictively used in the Sanskrit to refer to the sermons of the Buddha. In Chinese, the usage is broader and includes the works of the Sages.

15   Diamond (Vajracchedika) Sutra 金剛經
The complete name is 金剛般若波羅蜜經 , the Vajracchedika-prajnaparamita Sutra. It is a fundamental sutra of Buddhism and was first translated into the Chinese by Kumarajiva. The original is said to have been lost.

16   Eastern Ch'an Temple 東禪寺
The temple where the Fifth Patriarch lived. It was here that the Dharma was transmitted to Hui Neng. The place is one li (0.358 mile) southwest of Huang Mei District.

Footnotes

17 Ch'i Chou 薪州
An area in Hupeh, 湖北 , in which is Huang Mei County, 黃梅
縣 , where the Fourth and Fifth Patriarchs had lived.

18 District of Huang Mei 黃梅縣
The district in Ch'i Chou, 薪州 , in Hupeh.

19 Hung Jen 宏忍
The Fifth Patriarch, a native of Ch'i Chou, 薪州 , and the direct
antecedent in the patriarchate of Hui Neng, the Sixth Patriarch.
See lineage in Chapter X.

20 Ten taels 十兩
Ten ounces of silver.

21 Discriminating-alertness 智慧
The ability quickly, alertly to be aware of the virtuous versus the
erroneous thoughts as they arise from one's mind.

22 Field-of-merits 福田
The sphere of beneficial thoughts, motives and merits, the discipline
of the mind to retain only the virtuous thoughts. In its simpler meaning it carries with it a quality of self-discipline for the benefit of
the self. In its deeper implications it is a 'sphere of virtue for the
benefit of mankind', 為與衆生作福田 .

23 Prajna 般若
Total wisdom of the virtuous doctrines and the complete instantaneous
separation of the virtuous thoughts and motives from the erroneous.
It is a step beyond discriminating-alertness. It is wisdom plus its
proper function in an almost intuitive sense.

24 Shen Hsiu 神秀
Family name Lee, born in Tung Ching Wei, 東京尉 . He was a
disciple of the Fifth Patriarch and held the next highest position in
the monastery. (Through the patronage and high honors bestowed
upon him by the Empress Wu), he became the leader of the Gradual
School of Buddhism in Northern China. He died in 706 A.D.

25 Lu Chen 盧珍
A retired scholar and painter who gave his time and art to the monastery at Huang Mei.

26 Lankavatara Sutra 楞伽經
A series of discourses by Sakyamuni as delivered on the Lanka Mountains, 楞伽山 , in Ceylon. This was the sutra followed by Bodhi-
dharma---and is a recognized scripture of the Ch'an School.

27 Watch, third 三更
The night is divided into five watches of two hours each. The first
watch is from 7 P.M. to 9 P.M., and the third watch is from 11 P.M.
to 1 A.M. In contrast with this, in Biblical times, the watches are
divided into four periods of three hours each beginning at 6 P.M.

28 Bodhi tree 菩提樹
The wisdom tree, i.e. that under which the Buddha attained his final
enlightenment. A branch of it is said to have been sent by Asoka to
Ceylon from which sprang the celebrated Bo-tree still flourishing
there. (Recently, a cutting of this original tree has been transplanted
to the Buddha's Universal Church at 720 Washington Street, San
Francisco, California and is now growing there).

29 Enter the Gate 入門
To awaken to the truth and to practice it. It is more than just literal
knowledge of Buddhism. The literal knowledge without the practice
is still to be outside of the gate. This is used as a term for entrance
to deeper realization.

30 'All that has form is empty and vain' 凡所有相皆是虛妄
From the Diamond Sutra, Chapter V.

31 Boundless awakening 無上菩提
This phrase comes from two compounds, 無上 , unsurpassed, supreme, unexcelled; and 菩提 , bodhi or enlightenment. Together,
the meaning refers to the boundless awakening like the Buddha's.

32 Chiang Chou 江州
A district now part of Hupei, 湖北 , Province.

33 Bodhisattva, 菩薩 , refers to a Buddhist whose purpose is dedicated
not to his own salvation but to that of all mankind. Also, a person
who has attained Buddhahood but still lives like an ordinary person
so that he may help others find their way out of suffering. This is
considered to be a distinguishing characteristic of the Mahayana
School.

34 The rice symbolizes the Dharma. The sifting, to its actual practice. Thus, the real meaning of Hui Neng's answer is, "I have understood the Dharma for some time but I still need to put it into actual practice."

35 應無所住而生其心
Diamond Sutra, Chapter X. 金剛經第十.

36 Bodhidharma 達磨佛祖師
The twenty-eighth Indian and also the first Chinese patriarch, who arrived in China in 520 A.D. (He was the third son of a king in southern India.) He developed the Pristine School of Buddhism in China when he arrived at Canton and settled at Loyang, 洛陽.

37 Huai 懷集
A county of Kwangsi, 廣西, Province.

38 Hui refers to Szu Hui 四會
A county in Kwangtung.

39 Chiu Chiang 九江
Now a county in Kiangsi Province. Not to be confused with a district in Kwangtung, which is much further south.

40 Ta Yu Mountains 大庾嶺
In the southern part of Ta Yu County of Kiangsi Province, just north of Kwangtung.

41 Ch'en Hui Ming 陳惠明
One of the disciples of the Fifth Patriarch who was a descendant of Emperor Ch'en Hsuan, 陳宣, (578-580 A.D.) of the Northern Chou Dynasty. In ancient times, there were ten classes of generals. Ch'en was a fourth class general.

42 Original appearance 本來面目
The original, fundamental appearance, i.e. one's original nature which is inherently pure, calm and quiet. It is non-dual. It is uncluttered by the 'eighty-four thousand' anxieties.

43 Ts'ao Ch'i 曹溪
Ts'ao Ch'i is fifty li southeast of Ch'u Kiang, 曲江, district of Kwangtung Province. At this place, a person by the name of Ts'ao

Shu Liang, 曹叔良 , donated his home for the monastery. Since there was a stream (Ch'i, 溪) flowing nearby, the monastery was thus named Ts'ao Ch'i.

44 Szu Hui, 四會 ; 縣 , a county. See Footnote No. 38.

45 Fa Hsing Monastery 法性寺
This monastery is in the northwestern portion of the capitol of Kwang-tung Province. Originally there were two monasteries, Kan Ming, 乾明 , and Fa Hsing, 法性 . Later, the name was changed to 法性 . It is now known as the K'uan Hsiao Monastery, 光孝寺 .

46 Kwang Chou 廣州
An old geographical term – now Kwangtung and Kiangsi Provinces.

47 Nirvana Sutra 涅槃經
There are two versions, one the Hinayana, the other the Mahayana, both of which are translated into Chinese in several versions and there are numerous treatises on them; e.g. 佛般涅槃經 Mahapari-nirvana Sutra, translated by Po-Fa-tsu A.D. 290-306 of the Western Chin Dynasty, B.N. 552. 大般涅槃經 translated by Fa-hsien B.N. 118. The complete translation is 大般涅槃經 translated by Dharmaraksa A.D. 423 B.N. 113.

48 Raja Kao Kuei Te 高貴德王
A Bodhisattva in the time of the Buddha. In the Mahaparinirvana Sutra, Volumes 21 to 26 are called the 高貴德王品 the Raja Kao Kuei Te section.

49 Four inhibitions, 四重禁 , parajikas.
The four grave inhibitions or sins are: 殺 killing, 盜 stealing, 婬 carnality and 妄 lying.

50 Five misdeeds: 五逆罪 . (1) 不念父母養育恩典 . To forget our moral obligations to our parents for their benevolences on raising and educating us. (2) 不敬而害師長 . To be disrespectful and even to do harm to one's teachers. (3) 骨肉親情置若罔聞 . To turn a deaf ear to the problems and difficulties that one's brothers and sisters may have. (4) 鬧天鬧地鬧尊長忘恩負義 . To berate heaven, scold the earth, rebuke one's elders. To forget be-nevolences received, to be an ingrate. (5) 謗爛正教當平常 . To malign and to vilify religious beliefs without concern.

51 Buddha-nature, 佛性 , Buddhata, means the innate nature of enlightenment or Buddhahood within everyone. Though this potentiality
is inherent in all, it requires assiduous cultivation of the virtuous
roots to perfection before its fruit can ripen.

52 Five Skandhas, 五蘊 , the five aggregates, or components, or attributes of a person. (1) 色 , rupa, matter, form i.e. the physical
form as related to the five sense organs. (2) 受 , vedana, sensation, feeling, reception, the functioning of the mind in connection
with things. (3) 想 , sanjna, conception, or discernment, the function of the mind in distinguishing. (4) 行 , samskara, the functioning of the mind regarding likes and dislikes, good and evil. (5) 識 ,
vijnana, mental faculty, and knowledge, in regard to cognition and
perception, discriminative function in affairs and incidents.

53 Tung Shan School 東山法門
東山 , Tung Shan, in 湖南 , Hunan, where the Fourth Patriarch,
道信 , Tao Hsing, and the Fifth Patriarch, 宏忍 , Hung Jen, had
lived and where Hui Neng attained the patriarchate. So he called
his school after this site, therefore, the Tung Shan School.

CHAPTER II

PRAJNA

般若品

On the following day, the Prefect Wei requested further instructions. Having taken his seat, the Master addressed the large gathering saying, "Let everyone calm the thoughts of his mind and we will consider the Maha-prajna-paramita."[1]

"Virtuous and learned counselors," he continued, "the wisdom of prajna and of awakening is what ordinary people have naturally. It is only because their minds are deluded that they are unable to realize it for themselves, and thus need to resort to the very best of good and learned counselors to point out to them how to realize (their true) nature. You should understand that between the ignorant and the wise person, there is fundamentally no difference as to the Buddha-nature. It is only because of the varying degrees of delusion that they have different depths of realization. Thus, there are some who are ignorant and some who are wise.

"I am now going to talk to you about the doctrine of the Maha-prajna-paramita. If you put it into practice everyone of you will attain to the wisdom of prajna. So you must listen attentively with an undivided mind while I explain it to you.

"Virtuous and learned counselors, ordinary people recite prajna all day with their mouths, but they do not know that prajna is really within their self-nature. This is like (expecting the talk of) food to fill the stomach.

The mouth itself can speak only vanity, and by such means you cannot realize your own nature in ten thousand kalpas. [2] Fundamentally, it is of no benefit.

"Virtuous and learned counselors, Maha-prajna-paramita is a Sanskrit term meaning 'the great wisdom for crossing to that opposite shore'. [3] But this requires practice in one's mind rather than just saying it with one's mouth. To recite it with a mouth and not to practice it with the mind, is like a mirage, like a mere appearance, like dew, like lightning. But to recite it with the mouth and to practice it in the mind is to have the necessary harmony of mind and mouth. Our original nature is the Buddha and apart from our nature, there is no other Buddha.

"What is the meaning of this word 'maha'? Maha means great, as the capacity of the mind is great. It is like the infinite space in its retention of men and matters. It has no limits. It is not attainable by views that are square or round, big or little. It is not green or yellow, red or white; nor is it high or low, long or short; nor is it angry or happy, neither does it exist nor not exist. It is neither self-righteous nor critical of others. It does not have graduates or beginners. Such are all the Buddha-realms[4] which are also entirely identical with this infinite capacity of space. An ordinary person can attain this limitless, capacious nature (of the Buddha), but not through any single rigid method. The infinite capacity of a person's true self-nature is likewise attainable through this doctrine of suchness. [5]

"But virtuous and learned counselors, do not listen to this speaking of the void[6] and at once try to concentrate on emptiness. It is most essential that you do not concentrate on emptiness. For, if you misinterpret this spaciousness of the self-nature to be just sitting with an emptied, blank and vacuous mind, then you are actually manifesting the void of total amnesia.[7]

"Virtuous and learned counselors, the vastness of universal space can contain the ten thousand things of every shape, form, and symbolism - the sun, moon, and stars; the mountains and rivers, the great earth with its springs, streams, and waterfalls; grasses, trees, and thick forests; sinners and saints; the ways of the good and of the expedient; the heavens and the hells;[8] all the great oceans and Mt. Sumeru.[9] All these are in the void. The ordinary man's nature should be the void in just this way.

"Virtuous and learned counselors, if one's self-nature can contain the ten thousand things it is great, for the ten thousand things are within the nature of everyone. If one looks upon all people, evil or good, entirely without accepting or rejecting, and likewise without their sticking or adhering (to one's mind), then the mind has this capacity of space and we call it great. Hence this term maha.

"Virtuous and learned counselors, deluded people speak of it with their mouths, but the wise practice it with their minds. There are also deluded people who empty their minds and sit in silence thinking about absolutely nothing. Yet, they declare themselves to be great. But we can hardly induce these persons to change their attitude because their views are so distorted.

"Virtuous and learned counselors, the capacity of the mind is vast, completely pervading the dharmadhatu. [10] Use it, and immediately there is complete and clear-cut understanding. Rightly used, one then understands all things. For all things are one, and one is all. When they can come and go of themselves, and there is no stagnation in body or mind, then it is prajna.

29

"Virtuous and learned counselors, the whole wisdom of prajna comes entirely from our self-nature. It does not come from outside and enter into us. Make no mistake about this. This is the true functioning of our self-nature. This is the one reality (of suchness) towards all. The attainment of the limitless capacity of the mind is the doctrine of the mahayana;[11] so do not follow some one-sided, limited way. Do not merely talk of the void all day while not practicing it in your own mind. This would be as if a commoner were to proclaim himself king of the country. This is futile and such a one is not my student.

"Virtuous and learned counselors, what is the meaning of prajna? Translated into Chinese it means wisdom. At all times and places, whenever the momentary succession of our thoughts is not ignorant and we constantly practice wisdom...this is the working of prajna. With a single ignorant thought, prajna comes instantly to an end. With a single wise thought, prajna instantly arises. Ordinary people who are ignorant and deluded do not realize prajna. They render lip service to prajna with their mouths but their minds are constantly ignorant. They keep saying of themselves, 'I practice prajna'...and are talking continually about the void, but they do not know the real void. Prajna has neither shape, form, method, nor a way ...it is (the innate) wisdom of our minds. If this is the way you understand it, then you have the true meaning of prajna.

"What is the meaning of paramita? This is a Sanskrit term which in Chinese means 'reaching that opposite shore.' Its deeper meaning is the mind's prescinding of the starting and stopping of thoughts. When we attach our minds to circumstances, the starting and stopping (of thoughts) begins. It is like water churned by waves and this is to be on this shore. To let go of circumstances, to be without

30

the starting and stopping of thoughts, this is like water which ever flows on and is called that shore, hence the term paramita.

"Virtuous and learned counselors, deluded people say it with their mouths but while doing so, they are living an untruth. However, if it is put into practice from one moment's thought to another, this is called one's genuine nature. One who realizes this doctrine, is realizing the doctrine of prajna. One who practices this way, is practicing the way of prajna. Not to practice it is to be an ordinary person. To practice this way in just one thought means that oneself will be classified with the Buddhas.

"Virtuous and learned counselors, an ordinary man is a Buddha and defilements[12] are bodhi. With your thoughts under delusion, you are an ordinary person, but with your subsequent thoughts awakened, you become a Buddha. Your former thoughts attached to circumstances are defilements, but when the subsequent thoughts are prescinded from circumstances, it is bodhi.

"Virtuous and learned counselors, Maha-prajna-paramita is the supreme, the highest, the paramount doctrine. In it there is neither staying, going, nor yet coming. All the Buddhas of the three worlds evolve through it. One should use its great wisdom to shatter the five skandhas, the defilements, and the turmoil of the gunas.[13] If you practice in this way, you are certain to be perfect in Buddhism. You will change the three poisons (of greed, anger, and attachments) into discipline, equanimity, and wisdom.

"Virtuous and learned counselors, in my school and doctrine from this one (basis) of prajna arises the eighty-four thousand[14] kinds of wisdom. How can this be? Because ordinary people have eighty-four thousand ways of stirring up dust.[15] However, if you do not stir up dust, wisdom will always be manifest and you will not depart from self-nature. To realize this doctrine...this is precisely 'no-thought'. Do not recall (the past), do not dwell (in the present), do not construct phantasies (of the future), use the genuine suchness of your own nature and observe all matters with wisdom. Neither to grasp nor to avoid, this is to realize one's own nature and to attain Buddhahood.

"Virtuous and learned counselors, if you wish to enter the profoundest realm of the Dharma and (to experience) the prajna-samadhi itself, you must practice the way of prajna, by observing the Diamond Sutra. This will enable you to realize your self-nature directly. You should know that the virtuous merits (following the practice) of this sutra are immeasurable and limitless, and that the sutra itself most distinctly praises them in the highest terms. They are beyond words! The doctrines therein are the supreme vehicle and address themselves to those of great insight and superior endowment. When they are heard by those of little endowment and little insight they are incredulous. Why is this so?

"For example, if the sky-dragon should pour forth rain on the Jambudvipa,[16] the cities and villages would all be flooded and drift away like palm leaves. But if it should rain on the great ocean, the latter neither increases nor decreases. If a follower of the Mahayana of greatly superior endowment hears the words of the Diamond Sutra, he will realize them in his mind as soon as he hears them. (Such a one) naturally has the wisdom of prajna. Making use of this wisdom and always observing the reality without relying on words, he will thus know his own original nature. Actually, the rain water does not come from the sky, for its origin stems from the sky-dragon who is able to bring it forth so that all the people, all the plants and trees, and all the sentient creatures together can receive its refreshment. A hundred streams flow at last into the great ocean and are united in one body. The prajna wisdom, the original nature of ordinary people, is just like this.

"Virtuous and learned counselors, plants and trees with shallow roots are entirely upset when a big rain comes, and cannot grow any larger. It is the same with persons of little endowment when they hear this sudden doctrine. Basically, he has the prajna wisdom, and in this respect he is no different from a person of great wisdom. Then how is it that he hears the Dharma and does not naturally come to an awakening? The reason is that he has warped views, deep-rooted prejudices, heavy encumbrances, and anxieties. These are like huge clouds obscuring the sun; when there is no wind to blow them away, the sun's light does not appear.

"So, too, the prajna wisdom is neither great nor small, but it is only because of the delusions in people's own minds that they do not realize it alike. The deluded mind looks outside itself to seek the Buddha, not yet realizing that its own self-nature (will be the Buddha). This is to be of little endowment. If you are to be opened to a realization of the sudden school, do not be disposed towards external practices. But at all times, give rise only to such perfect views within one's mind itself, that anxieties and cares are ever unable to contaminate[17] them. Thus, one realizes one's nature.

"Virtuous and learned counselors, do not abide within or without. Let (your thoughts) come and go freely. If you are able to get rid of the prejudiced mind...if you can understand thoroughly without any obstructions...if you can practice the Dharma in this way, then it (your mind) is basically no different from the Prajna Sutra.

"Virtuous and learned counselors, all the sutras and all the literature of the greater and lesser vehicles, as well as the twelve divisions of the canon were formulated because of the peoples' needs! Hence, according to your wisdom will your nature attain a firm and correct understanding. If there were no people, all of the ten thousand methods [18] would not have arisen. Therefore, one should know that the ten thousand methods arose because of the needs of the people for them. All the sutras and literature came about because of the causal affinity with the people. Under these conditions, of course, there will be men who are ignorant and others who are wise...the ignorant of little capacity and the wise of great.

"When ignorant people ask questions of the wise, the wise discusses the doctrine with the ignorant. If the ignorant man can suddenly attain an awakening, and if his mind is opened immediately, then he is no different from the wise. Virtuous and learned counselors, if there is not an awakening then a Buddha is just an ordinary person. But if there is an awakening, in one moment's thought, the ordinary person is Buddha. Knowing then that the ten thousand methods are all in the mind itself, why do you not from within the mind itself instantly see into the true suchness of the self-nature.

"The Bodhisattva Sila Sutra [19] says, 'Our self-nature is originally clear and quiet. If we realize the mind itself and see into its nature, we should all attain Buddhahood.' The Vimalakirti Sutra [20] says, 'In the instant of complete and receptive comprehension, the clarity and quietness of the original mind appears.'

34

"Virtuous and learned counselors, when I was with the Fifth Patriarch, I had only to hear of it to awaken instantly and to perceive at once the true suchness of my original nature. Therefore, I have come to propagate the doctrine of this school, by which a student of the Dharma can awaken instantly to bodhi...by each looking into his own mind and seeing within himself his own original nature. If you do not realize it for yourself, you should seek out a wise counselor who will explain the supreme doctrine and direct you into the right path.

"Such a wise counselor will have a great causal affinity with you. For what we call counseling is to teach and guide (a person) to attain the realization of his nature, and that is why a wise counselor has to be able to apply all the proper methods skillfully. All the Buddhas of the three worlds[21] as well as the twelve divisions of the canon are within our self-nature; from the beginning they are there in their entirety, and yet one may not be able to realize it for oneself. It is then necessary to seek out a wise counselor to point it out before realization is possible.

"But if one has realized by oneself, one need not rely on outside help. However, if a person still has prejudices but states that because of the wisdom of his counselor he will be able to attain liberation...such a view is also groundless. Why is this so? One's mind does have the wisdom to realize itself, but if you do not cease giving rise to prejudices, delusions, baseless and confused thoughts, then, even though you have been taught by a wise counselor, your liberation is still impossible. However, if your observation is done with virtuous views, suchness, and prajna, all baseless thoughts will come to an end in an instant. If you know your self-nature, upon realizing it, you will directly attain Buddhahood.

35

"Virtuous and learned counselors, by observing one's thoughts with prajna, completely understanding them within and without, one can know one's original mind. If one knows the original mind, then one is basically liberated. If one attains liberation, then one attains the tranquil-equanimity of prajna which is 'no-thought'.

"What does 'no-thought' mean? If you see anything and your mind is not contaminated by or attached to it... this is called 'no-thought'. You should practice this everywhere and yet not be attached anywhere. You have only to quiet the original mind so as to have the six senses flowing through their six orifices to come into contact with the six qualities without contamination and without distraction, the thoughts coming and going of themselves, for through the use of wisdom there is no blockage. This is the tranquil-equanimity of prajna and natural liberation. [22] Such is the practice of 'no-thought'. But if you do not think of anything at all, and immediately command thoughts to cease, should they arise, this is to be tied in a knot by the doctrine [23] and is called an obtuse view.

"Virtuous and learned counselors, one who realizes the doctrine of 'no-thought' understands entirely the ten thousand things. One who realizes the doctrine of 'no-thought' sees all the Buddha realms. One who realizes the doctrine of 'no-thought' attains Buddhahood.

"Virtuous and learned counselors, should those of future generations who receive my doctrines, practice this discipline of the sudden school with others of the same views, and should they also vow to cherish the teachings, as if they were serving the Buddha himself for all their lives without turning back, then they certainly may attain the rank of sages. Though it has been necessary to transmit the teachings from previous Patriarchs down to the pre-

36

sent by esoteric transmission of instructions, yet we do not hide the true doctrines.

"To those who do not hold the same views or practices, or who belong to a different persuasion, do not transmit the instructions. Such action is not only derogatory to the original preceptors, but also would bring no ultimate benefit. I fear that there may be ignorant ones without understanding who will speak ill of our doctrine, and thus for a hundred kalpas and a thousand lives smother the seeds of Buddha-nature.

"Virtuous and learned counselors, I have a poem-of-the-formless which all of you should understand and recite whether you are laymen or monks. But be sure to practice it, for if you do not practice it for yourselves, it will be valueless just to remember the words alone.

"Listen to my poem:

To speak with comprehension and to comprehend
    also in the mind,
Is to be like the sun in the clear sky.

By receiving the transmission of the doctrine
    of seeing into our self-nature,
We are able to be delivered from this world,
    and to abolish prejudiced ideas.

The doctrine in itself is neither fast nor slow.
There is only fastness and slowness in peoples'
    transition from delusion to awakening.

But as to this way of seeing into one's nature,
Even the most ignorant person cannot say he
    does not understand.

Though the doctrine is explained through ten
    thousand approaches,
The final principle is ultimately but one.

Even more so in the midst of the dark hours of
    anxieties,
We should have ever arising, the sunlight of
    wisdom.

With biased views, anxieties appear.
But with virtuous views, the anxieties disappear.

When we need use neither biased nor virtuous
    views,
Then there is purity and tranquility without
    blemish.

Bodhi is originally within our self-nature,
But if we have the idea that we have it, we
    are at once deluded.

In the midst of delusions, quiet the mind by
    not pursuing them,
For only the clear virtuous mind is beyond the
    three hindrances.[24]

When people practice the Dharma,
They should allow nothing to stand in their way.

If we search continuously for our own errors,
We shall be in unity with the Dharma.

All creatures have their own Dharma naturally,
And each is not an obstruction to the other.

But if the people neglect their inward Dharma

and seek it elsewhere,
They will go through their entire lives without
realizing the Dharma.

If we allow our lifetime to go by like the waves
aimlessly,
In the end we will have nothing but self-
reproach.

If we want to attain the realization of the
genuine Dharma,
Virtuous practice will lead us directly to it.
However, if we have no mind for the Dharma,
We will be walking in the gloom and not see it.

If we truly practice the Dharma,
We will not find fault anywhere.
If we see the deficiencies of others,
Our criticisms are in themselves manifestations
of our own faults.

Others may be wrong, but we do not criticize,
For if we criticize we are already at fault.

We have only to be rid of our censorious minds
To start abolishing our defilements and anxieties.

When the mind is no longer concerned with
likes and dislikes,
Then it can be at ease, as if we were asleep
with our legs fully stretched.

If we want to be able to help others,
We must ourselves have the open-minded
helpfulness.[25]

In order not to allow others to harbor doubts,
Our own self-nature must be absolutely clear
of them.

The Dharma of Buddhism is used in the midst
of our usual life,
And thus is not separate from our usual consciousness.

To seek for wisdom by shedding one's personal
responsibilities,
Is to be seeking for the horns of a rabbit.

Virtuous views are the liberating ones.
Biased views tether us to this world.
When we have entirely abolished the biased
views and also purified the virtuous ones,
Then the wisdom of the self-nature will fully
appear.

This poem is of the sudden school,
And is also called – The Great Dharma Ship.

The deluded ones may have listened many
times to the sutras,
But this will not rid them of the multitudinous
hindrances.
However, in awakening to Bodhi wisdom, they
are instantly in accord with the Dharma.

"The Master went on saying, 'Today at Ta Fan Monastery, I have explained this sudden doctrine. May all
beings in this Dharma world, at these words, see into their
true natures and become Buddhas.'

"When Prefect Wei and his officials, the Taoists, and

40

laymen had heard the Master's words, there was not one of them whose mind was not awakened. With one accord they paid their respects, saying, 'This is indeed wonderful! Who would have thought that a Buddha would come to life in Ling Nan.'"

FOOTNOTES

1   Maha-prajna-paramita 摩訶般若波羅蜜多
    Maha, 摩訶 , great; prajna, 般若 , wisdom; paramita, 波羅
    蜜多 , derived from parama, the highest, the acme; thus, Maha-
    prajna-paramita means the great wisdom method of reaching that op-
    posite shore i.e. complete enlightenment.

2   Kalpa 刼
    An eon, age, a fabulous period of time, also a lifetime.

3   Opposite shore 彼岸
    In contrast to the Samsara life of a continuous round of births and
    deaths which is this shore, 此岸 , the opposite shore is the complete
    repayment of the karmic debts and the attainment of the enlighten-
    ment of a Buddha.

4   Buddha-realms, 佛剎土 , also, Buddhaksetra. The spiritual realm
    of one who has attained perfect enlightenment. It is vast and limit-
    less like the 'capacity of space'.

5   Suchness, 如 , tatha. Literally, so, thus, in such a manner, like,
    as. In Buddhism it is used as the reality, the suchness of all things-
    -the nature of things as it is. It is used frequently with, 真 , gen-
    uine, true, (or this word is implied) in combination as, 真如 ,
    bhutatathata. In this sense it means the ultimate reality, the abso-
    lute which is to be found in the self-nature.
    It is also commonly used as in, 如是 , 如是 , 是 , meaning is;
    being; so that the words together imply, 'as it is, so it is'. The in-
    ference being that we accept all things as they are without distorting
    them by our own ingrained prejudices and biases.

6   Void, emptiness, 空 , sunya. There are several meanings to this
    term. One is that one empties the mind, so that it is completely
    silent and thus to think of nothing. This, the Sixth Patriarch has
    said, is a deluded, a warped view.
    Void as used here, refers to the mind being like the emptiness of
    space in which all things can be contained, yet there is not a single
    thing to which one becomes attached. The limitless space represents
    the breadth of the person's heart and mind in regards to all matters.
    It refers to the greatness of the tranquility of a person's mind which
    is never disturbed by any innate or acquired attachment.

7   'Void of total amnesia' 無記空

無 , no, not, none; 記 , memory, remember; 空 , void. This means a void wherein one rejects all memory of one's experiences. Thus it is not void for it is still filled with 無記 , 'forget'---'do not remember'. Actually, one should not have this nor even have 'void' as such in one's mind.

8 Hells, 地獄 , naraka. The Buddhist hells are purgatories and not permanent hells as in some other religious interpretations. That is, they are abodes for the expiation of misdeeds. The duration of time is dependent on the number and severity of the infractions.

9 Mt. Sumeru 須彌山
Said to be the central and the highest mountain of every world. Used often to represent a huge quantity. But in this case used to represent incidents wherein one encounters tremendous egotism.

10 Dharmadhatu 法界
(1) A term used sometimes for all noumenal or phenomenal things.
(2) A term also used for a person's being open to Buddha-wisdom as, 開法界 , or opening one's own dharma-realm after one has attained enlightenment.

11 Mahayana, 大乘 , the great vehicle. Of particular interest is the use of this term in the Chinese terminology to mean a person of great capacity, great breadth and depth of mind. Beyond intelligence, it refers to compassion, to service for and in the interest of mankind.

12 Defilements, 煩惱 , klesa, the worries, troubles, and cares of the emotions and of one's ignorance which disturbs and beclouds the mind. As in the 'three poisons', 貪 , 瞋 , 癡 , greed, anger, and attachments, which are the roots from which the many varieties of anxieties arise.

13 Gunas, the six gunas, 六塵 , the six qualities produced by objects and the organs of sense, i.e. sight, sound, smell, taste, touch, idea. 塵 , is dust or dirt. These six qualities are therefore the cause of the impurities.

14 Eighty-four thousand 八萬四千
A term frequently used to mean an extremely large quantity, beyond counting, as eighty-four thousand kinds of wisdom.

43

15 Dust 塵勞

塵 , means small particles, dust, defilement, from which the two words mean the troubles of the everyday world, the passions.

16 Jambudvipa 閻浮提

Refers to the large continent south of Mt. Meru. Also an ancient name for the continent of Asia.

17 Contaminate 染

To dye, to be infected with, used for the defilements, the worries. If one has such anxieties in one's mind, it is said that he has been contaminated by them, and thus cannot realize his self-nature.

18 Ten thousand methods 萬法

In this passage, the term, 萬法 , refers to ten thousand methods and not things. It refers to all the different ways of expounding the doctrines in "all the sutras and all the literature, ---".

19 Bodhisattva Sila Sutra 菩薩戒經

The Sutra of the Rules of the Bodhisattva, is actually the, 菩薩心 地戒品第十 , the Rules of the Bodhisattva Mind, Section Ten, 卷二 , Volume 2 of the 梵網經 , Brahmajala Sutra translated by Kumarajiva, 406 A.D. into Chinese.

20 Vimalakirti Sutra, or the Vimalakirti-nirdesa Sutra, 淨明經 or the, 維摩詰經 . Vimalakirti was a native of Vaisali, 毘耶離 . He was contemporary with the Buddha and a devoted student of Buddhism. The sutra recorded his conversations with some residents of Vaisali, but particularly with the ten leading disciples of the Buddha. This was translated by Kumarajiva into the Chinese. The conversations demolished many erroneous concepts of the practice of Buddhism.

21 Three worlds 三世

Refers to three periods, the past, 過去 , the present, 現在 , and the future, 未來 .

22 Natural liberation, 自在解脫 , sahaja. Natural liberation is regarded as the original, pure state of the mind. When thoughts are free in one's mind, that is, without any hindrances or attachments, then it is in its natural state i.e., 自在 . Liberation i.e., 解脫 .

44

23 'Tied in a knot by the doctrine' 法縛
    This means that one, not understanding the doctrine in its fullest as-
    pect, may become so involved in a particular aspect of it, that in-
    stead of progressive enlightenment, one becomes tied in a knot to
    the point of stagnation by one's own gun-barrel vision.

24 Three hindrances, 三障 , the three vighna. These hindrances or
    barriers are first, 煩惱 ; 障 , the anxieties or the passions; second,
    業障 , the erroneous or evil actions that have been done; third,
    報障 , the retributions.

25 Proper means, 方便 , upaya. The Chinese, 方 , is used as, 方
    術 , skillful or adept method; 便 , as, 便用 , opportune, or ap-
    propriate use. So the complete term is interpreted as the appropriate
    use of skillful methods suitable to the particular circumstances in
    which one is helping others. Thus the methods are flexible but the
    doctrine is the same.

CHAPTER III

THE DISPELLING OF DOUBTS
疑問品

One day the Prefect Wei summoned a great gathering with the Master to partake of a meatless meal. At the end of the meal, the Prefect invited the Master to take the throne and together with the civil officials, scholars, and lay-folk, respectfully addressed him saying, "We have heard you explain the doctrine which, in fact, cannot be thought or put into words. We still have some minor doubts and wish that you, in your great compassion, would particularly explain them for us."

"The Master replied, 'If you have any doubts, just ask and I will immediately explain.'

"The Lord Wei then said, 'Is not that which you have expounded, the doctrine of the Great Master Bodhidharma?'

"Yes," said the Master.

"I have heard," said the Prefect, "that when Bodhidharma first began to convert Emperor Wu of Liang,[1] the Emperor asked him saying, 'Throughout my lifetime, I have built temples, assisted the monks, made contributions to them and fed them. What merit-virtue[2] have I gained?' Bodhidharma replied, 'In reality, there is no merit-virtue.' I do not yet understand this principle and I wish you would explain it to me."

"The Master answered, 'Of course there is no merit-virtue。 Do not doubt the words of the Old Sage。 The Emperor Wu's mind was misdirected; he did not understand the true doctrine. To build temples, assist the monks, make contributions and prepare meatless meals, these are called seeking good fortune[3] and one must not confuse good fortune with merit - virtue。 In the Dharmakaya,[4] merit-virtue does not consist of working for good fortune。' The Master went on, 'To realize one's nature is merit; to be even-minded is virtue。 When there is no blocking in the stream of thought, when you continually realize the original nature, when you do this truly, actually and profoundly, it is called merit-virtue。 Inward humility of the mind is merit; graciousness in conduct is virtue. To have the self-nature as the firm foundation of the ten thousand dharmas is merit; when the mind in its entirety is not clinging to thought, this is virtue。 Not to wander from one's self-nature is merit; responding to conditions without attachment is virtue。 If you seek to have merit-virtue in accord with the Dharmakaya, you have only to follow this method。 For this is the true merit-virtue.

'If there is one who is practicing merit-virtue, he is never disparaging in his thoughts but acts always with universal respect。 A mind always disparaging others is not free from egotism. This is naturally to be without merit. If one's own nature is under delusion and not realized, this is naturally to be without virtue, for the fact is that one's ego of itself is naturally grandiose。 It is always looking down on things。

'Therefore, learned and virtuous counselors, when thoughts flow without blocking, this is merit; when the mind is working in equanimity, this is virtue. The discipline of self-nature is merit; the discipline of one's own body is virtue. To have merit-virtue, you must see within your self-nature: you do not attain it by charity to monks.

48

Therefore, the virtue of fortune is different from the merit-virtue. The Emperor Wu did not understand the true principle, and it was not our Patriarch Master (Bodhidharma) who was in error.'

"The Prefect asked again, saying, 'I often see monks and laymen reciting the 'Amitabha'[5] wishing to be born in the Western Paradise.[6] Would Your Reverence please discuss this? Can one be born there or not? I would like you to dispel my doubts.'

"The Master said, 'Mr. Prefect, please listen carefully to what I have to say to you. In the city of Sravasti,[7] the Buddha spoke the sutra which gave instructions concerning the Western Paradise and made it plain that the journey there is not a matter of distance. From the literal standpoint, it is said to be ten 'wan' (ten thousand) and eight thousand li away, but this actually refers to the ten evils[8] and the eight delusions[9] within ourselves, and this is what is meant by speaking of it as distance. It may be called far away because of one's shallow roots. It may be called near because of one's lofty understanding. Though there are these two kinds of people, there are not two kinds of Dharmas. People differ in the time between delusion and awakening, for there is slowness and quickness in realization. Deluded people invoke the name Amitabha seeking to be born there (i.e., the Western Paradise) but an awakened person himself quiets the mind. Therefore, the Buddha says, 'When one's mind has become quiet, then there is the peace of Buddhahood.'

"Mr. Prefect, a person may be in the East, but if his mind be quiet, then there is no fault. But even though a person may be in the West, if his mind is not quiet, then he is still in error. Here is a person in the East. He is at fault and invokes the name of the Amitabha, seeking to

49

be born in the Western Paradise. Here is a person already in the West. He too is at fault, but where can he seek to be reborn by invoking the Amitabha name?

"Ignorant people do not understand their self-nature and do not know that the Land of Peace is within their own bodies, and thus wish to go East or wish to go West. But to the awakened person all places are alike. Therefore, the Buddha says, 'Be content with and enjoy whatever place you are in.' Let nothing unworthy enter or arise in the ground of your mind, Mr. Prefect, and then you will go in this way to a Western Paradise which is not distant. But if you harbor an unvirtuous mind, though you invoke the name of the Buddha, it will be difficult to be reborn there.

"Now, I would advise all the learned and virtuous counselors that first by removing the ten evils, you will have walked a hundred thousand li, and then when you remove the eight errors, you will have completed the remaining eight thousand. When you realize the true nature in every thought and constantly practice equanimity, you will get there in a snap of the fingers and thus behold Amitabha. All you have to do is to practice the ten virtues,[10] so, why need you seek further to be born in the Western Paradise? If you have not made an end of the ten evils in your mind, what Buddha will give you welcome? If you can but realize the non-arising of thoughts of the sudden doctrine, seeing the Western Paradise would take only an instant. But, if, without realization, one invokes the name of Amitabha to seek the way to be reborn in a distant land, how can one possibly attain it?

"I, and all of you, can arrive at the Western Paradise in the fraction of an instant and see it right before our eyes. Do you all wish to see?"

"Everyone respectfully said, 'If we can see it here, why should we have a wish for a future birth there? We wish that Your Reverence, out of your compassion and forbearance, would reveal the Western Paradise so that all can see it.'

"The Master said, 'The physical body of every ordinary person is a city of which the eyes, ears, nose and tongue are the gates. On the outside, there are the five gates, and within, is the gate of the intellect. The mind is the site, and the self-nature is the king who dwells upon the ground of the mind. When the self-nature is there, the king is there; when it departs, the king departs. When it is there, the mind and the body are alive, but when it departs, the mind and body decay. Buddhahood comes from cultivation of the self-nature within us. Do not seek it outside the body. When your self-nature is under delusion, you are ordinary people, but when your self-nature is awakened and alert, you are Buddhas.

'To have compassion and forbearance is Avalokitesvara.[11] Cheerfulness and charity are called Mahasthamaprapta.[12] To be at peace is Sakyamuni.[13] To be even-minded is Amitabha. The distinction of yours-and-mine is Mt. Meru. Erroneous thinking is the water of the ocean, and passions are the waves. The desire to injure others is the evil dragon. Idle thoughts are the demons. Worldly cares are the fishes and turtles. Greed and anger are the purgatories. Stupidities and attachments are the animals.

'Virtuous and learned counselors, constantly practice the ten virtues and the heaven-world appears. Remove the distinction of yours-and-mine and Mt. Meru is overturned. Do away with erroneous thoughts and the ocean is dried up. Get rid of the passions and the worries and the waves subside. Forget the desire to injure and the fishes and the dragons die. When within the ground of your own mind you are awakened to the nature of such-ness, there shines forth a great brightness, radiating through the six sense-gates clearly and serenely, dispersing the six spheres of desire. When the self-nature is inwardly radi-ating, the three poisons are at once removed; the purga-tories and all the evil deeds are directly dissipated. To understand clearly thus within and without, is not different from being in the Western Paradise. But, if you do not practice this discipline, how can you reach it?'

"Hearing these words, all those present immediately saw into their true nature and paid profound respect to the Master, praising, 'Marvelous, indeed, is this!

'We make an all-embracing vow,' they chanted, 'that beings in all the Dharma worlds shall hear this teach-ing and directly attain realization.'

"The Master said, 'If you wish to practice, you can do so while living with your family.[14] It is not necessary to go to a monastery. To be able to practice while being with one's family is to be like an Easterner with a pure mind. To be in a monastery and yet not to practice is to be like a Westerner with an evil mind. The mind has only to be clear and quiet and thus one's self-nature is in the Western Paradise.'

"The Prefect Wei asked again, 'How can one practice while living with one's family? I wish you would give us some instructions.'

"The Master replied, 'I have a poem of the formless for all of you. You have only to put it into practice and you will always be in just the same place as I (i.e., you will be in this monastery where I teach). However, if you

52

do not put it into practice, you may shave your hair and leave your family, but of what benefit will it be to your practice of the Dharma?

"The poem says:

If the mind is in a state of equanimity,
    what is the need of observing the precepts?

If you are straightforward in mind,
    what is the use of practicing dhyana?[15]

The life of gratitude is the personal tending of
    father and mother.

The life of generosity is to sympathize equally
    with superiors and inferiors.

The life of deference is being at peace with both
    seniors and juniors.

The life of patience is not to bicker when others
    are at fault.

If you can get fire from drilling wood,
    then the red lotus will certainly arise from
    the mud.

That which tastes bitter in the mouth is really
    soothing medicine;
What jars the ear is actually sincere speech.

In abandoning errors, prajna inevitably will arise,
    but to defend one's defects reveals an ig-
    noble mind.

Always spend your days in forgiveness and generosity, for the attainment of the Dharma is
not just in giving money.

You will find bodhi only within the mind, so of
what use is it to seek the mystery outside?

If you listen to my teaching and accord with its
practice, heaven is right before your eyes.

"The Master again said, 'Virtuous and learned counselors, it is only necessary for you to put this poem into
practice and you will attain the vision of self-nature and
directly realize Buddhahood. Do not delay to practice the
Dharma. All of you can now leave as I am returning to
Ts'ao Ch'i. If anyone has any doubts, he can come and
ask about them.'"

At that time, the Prefect Wei, his officials, and the
virtuous men and faithful women who were at the gathering, all attained an opening of realization, believing,
accepting, and following the practice.

FOOTNOTES

1. Emperor Wu of Liang 梁武帝
   Reigned as Emperor of China for a period of forty-eight years 502-550 A.D., during the Liang Dynasty which lasted from 502 A.D. to 556 A.D.

2. Merit-virtue 功德
   功 , merit, meritorious; 德 , virtue, moral excellence. In Buddhist terminology this has some special implications. 功德 , merit-virtue, implies not only that benevolent actions are done without any expectation of reward but also the inward merits which pertain to the freeing of one's mind from all attachments, delusions, and erroneous views back to its original, pristine status of clarity and quietude. This is frequently confused as did Emperor Wu with, 福 , wealth, 德 , virtue. This is the usual performance of good deeds to which are attached some degree of expectation of reward. Since this reward is usually in good fortune, it is called, 福德 , to which we shall apply the term 'karmic-virtue'. But the most important fact is that there is not an accompanying discipline of the mind in these activities so they cannot be called, 功德 merit-virtue, which is the point of the Patriarch's discussion. To clarify these distinctive points, we are using the full terms of merit-virtue for 功德 rather than just merits, because it is important that these differences be clearly understood.

3. Seeking good fortune 求福
   The performance of good deeds by which one seeks a reward in our mundane existence.

4. Dharmakaya 法身

5. Amitabha 阿彌陀佛
   Refers to the Buddha of infinite qualities. One of these qualities is the tranquility of the mind. He has always been associated with the West and from this came the conception of a Western Paradise. It is believed by some that the repetition of his name will result in some aid in tranquilizing the person's own mind. The extension of this disciplinary aid led many people to believe that the continual repetition of the name alone will result in one's being born in the Western Paradise. Of course, the Sixth Patriarch disproved this point.

6. Western Paradise, 西方 , has general reference to the site of the Buddhist heaven. Interestingly enough, the origin of the term came

55

from the Buddha's own travelling westward when he left the palace to seek and to attain enlightenment. He continued West as he spoke. So Western Paradise is also synonymous with the attainment of enlightenment or the attainment of Buddhahood.

7 Sravasti 舍衛城
An ancient city and kingdom five hundred li northwest of Kapilavastu, now Rapetmapet, south of the Rapti River. It is said to have been in Northern Kosala. The Jetavana, 祇園 , was located there.

8 Ten evils 十惡
Dasakusala, the ten evils are: 殺生 killing; 偷盜 stealing; 邪婬 adultery; 妄語 fabrication; 兩舌 double-tongue; 惡口 evil mouth; 綺語 coarse language; 貪慾 greed; 嗔恚 anger; 邪見 biased views.

9 Eight delusions 八邪
Refers to the eight improper, or biased practices, the opposite of the eight virtues, 八正道 .

10 Ten virtues 十善
The ten good characteristics or virtues; it is defined as the abstinence of thoughts of the ten evils -- (see ten evils 十惡). 十善 is also 孝 filial devotion; 悌 brotherhood; 忠 loyalty; 信 trustworthiness; 禮 graciousness; 義 generosity; 廉 frugality; 恥 humility; 節 determination; and 基地 foundation.

11 Avalokitesvara, 觀音 , also, 觀世音 . 觀 to observe, to regard; 世 , the world; 音 , the sounds; observer of the world's sounds or cries. This is the name of the Merciful Bodhisattva, Kuan-Yin, often erroneously referred to as the Goddess of Mercy. Kuan-Yin is the one on the left of the triad of Amida, while Mahasthamaprapta is on the right.

12 Mahasthamaprapta 勢至
勢 , bala, sthaman, power, influence, authority; aspect, circumstances. 勢至 He, whose wisdom and power reaches everywhere, Mahasthamaprapta, i.e. 大勢至 , great power arrived (at maturity). It is also the name of the Bodhisattva on the right of Amitabha.

13 Sakyamuni 釋迦牟尼
釋迦 , Sakya, the name of the clan of the Buddha---muni is sage;

so Sakyamuni is the Buddha, or the 'sage of the Sakya clan'. He was the son of Suddhodana, the ruler of Kapilavastu on the slopes of the Nepalese hills. His mother was Maya who died when the Buddha was seven days old. He was raised by her sister Prajapati.

14 "If you wish to practice, you can do so while living with your family"
若欲修行在家亦得
This statement and the poem of the formless which the Patriarch sub-sequently gives, emphasize the fact that a person may practice Bud-dhism without being in a monastery, for, in fact, Buddhism is a way of every day life. This principle seems to have been forgotten by many people and thereby an erroneous concept has risen---that one can only be a true Buddhist by leaving one's family. See also dis-cussion of this in the Vimalakirti Sutra.

15 Dhyana, 坐禅 , meditation; Dhyana a method of meditation where-in one sits quietly until his mind becomes calm and peaceful. The purpose is to understand and to be alert to the most minute thought in one's mind, to gain an equanimity that can be carried through to the next day, and to gain more enlightenment into one's daily ac-tivities to see how every incident can be more beneficial to others.

CHAPTER IV

EQUANIMITY AND WISDOM
定慧品

The Master said to the assembly, "Virtuous and learned counselors, my school takes equanimity[1] and wisdom
as its foundation. You should all avoid the mistake of saying that equanimity and wisdom are different. Equanimity
and wisdom are basically one - they are not two. Equanimity is the basis of wisdom. Wisdom is the function of
equanimity. When there is wisdom, equanimity is within
it. When there is equanimity, wisdom is within it. If you
are aware of what this means, then the knowledge of equanimity and wisdom is one and the same. Students of the
Dharma must not say that equanimity arises before wisdom
or that wisdom arises before equanimity as if they were
distinct. One who holds such views is making the Dharma
dualistic.

"When there is virtue in the mouth but not in the
mind, equanimity and wisdom are vain and are by no means
identical. But if there is virtue in both mind and mouth,
and if the internal and external are as one, equanimity and
wisdom are identical. When you are engaged in self-realization do not be involved in argument. If you argue about
which precedes and which follows, you are just like a deluded person; you have not freed yourself from gain and
loss; you are just aggravating your egotism and not dis-
carding the four perspectives.[2]

"Virtuous and learned counselors, to what shall we
compare equanimity and wisdom? They are like the light

Having the lamp you can have light, but with , there must be darkness, because the lamp is the basis of the light and the light is the use of the lamp. Though there are two names, their basis are the same. The doctrine of wisdom and equanimity is just like this.

"The Master said to the assembly, 'One who practices equanimity single-mindedly, does so in all places. Whether walking or standing, sitting or lying down, he continually maintains a single and straightforward mind. This is the point.'

"In the words of the Vimalakirti Sutra,[3] 'Straightforwardness of mind is the place of awakening; straightforwardness of mind is tranquility.'

"Do not have flattery and deceit in your mind and straightforwardness only in the words of the mouth. Just to talk about the single-minded practice of equanimity is not yet practicing straightforwardness of mind. You have only to practice straightforwardness of mind with respect to all types of doctrines without partiality and attachment. Deluded people attached to the mere letter of the doctrine, have a partial view of the single-minded equanimity. They describe it narrowly as 'Sitting without motion' and erroneously say 'that it is having no thoughts.' Those who understand it in this way are just like inanimate objects. This is a serious obstacle to affinity with the Dharma.

"Virtuous and learned counselors, the Dharma is essentially free-flowing, so why obstruct it in this way? When the mind does not dwell on any method, the Dharma is at once flowing freely. If the mind dwells upon any method, one is tying oneself up in knots. If one says that the point is to sit without moving, and without thinking,

then one is like Sariputra[4] who was reproved by Vimalakirti for practicing such dhyana in the forest.

"There are also people who teach that merits are to
be attained by sitting and watching the mind, until it is
in total stillness, without moving or any thoughts arising.
In their lack of understanding, such deluded ones become
mentally unbalanced by their one-sidedness. All such
people are mere formalists, and you should realize that
this is a great error.

"Virtuous and learned counselors, in the original and
orthodox teaching, there is no distinction between the
sudden and gradual school. It is just that peoples' natures
are sharp or dull. Deluded people understand gradually,
but awakened people understand and apply the teachings
instantly. But when any people know their original mind
and see into their original nature for themselves, then
there are no differences between them. Therefore, it is
really a nomenclature of expediency in the setting up of
the distinction between the sudden and gradual school.

'No - form'

"Virtuous and learned counselors, this doctrine of
mine, from its original inception, first established 'no-
thought' (無念) as its principle, 'no-form' (無相) as
its essence, 'no-abiding' (無住) as its foundation. The
doctrine of 'no-form' is to be involved in forms and yet to
be detached from form. The doctrine of 'no-thought' is to
be involved in thinking yet is to have no biased thoughts.

"The doctrine of 'no-abiding' is man's original nature. It is to treat this world's virtues and vices, joys and
sorrows, even enemies and kinsmen, and irritating, cutting, critical, and combative words as void...all without
any thought of retaliation. As thought follows thought, do
not think of the past. For if your past, present, and future

no — abiding

thoughts are not prevented from becoming a reciprocal series, it is called being tied in a knot. Under all circumstances and occurrences as one does not abide or dwell upon the thoughts as they follow each other, then there will certainly be no knot. This is what is meant by 'no-abiding' as the foundation.

"Virtuous and learned counselors, to be detached from external forms is called 'no-form.' To be able to be thus detached while involved in forms is the clarity and calmness which are the very basis of the Dharma. This is why we take 'no-form' as our essence.

"In all situations, when the mind is not discolored by any biased views then it is called the state of 'no-thought.' While engaged in one's thinking, continuously dispose of each situation without letting any egoistic thoughts arise. But if you take this to mean that you do not think of anything at all...that thoughts should be completely eradicated, and then, when every thought has ceased, to die and be born in the Western Paradise...this is a tremendous mistake. Students of the Dharma should consider this well.

"If you do not understand the meaning of the Dharma and are yourself in error, this is understandable.[5] But when you persuade others with these errors, then you not only are blind to your own delusions but are also corrupting the sutras. This is why we establish 'no-thought' as our principle.

— No-thought 'principle

"Virtuous and learned counselors, how is it that we take 'no-thought' as our principle? Under circumstances where one is only talking about seeing into one's nature, the deluded person is possessed by thoughts while in the midst of situations. These thoughts arise to form biased views and from these come further defilements and irrelevant thoughts. In understanding our self-nature, from the beginning one must realize there is not one single doctrine, or method, to be attained. If you imagine that there is something to be attained, there immediately arises irrelevant talk of successes and failures, and these are precisely defilements and biased views. That is why our school sets up 'no-thought' as our principle.

"Virtuous and learned counselors, 'no', as in 'no-thought', is 'no what?' 'Thought' itself is thinking of what? 'No' is non-duality; the absence of every type of defiled thinking. Then 'thought' becomes the thinking of the real suchness of our original nature. This real suchness is in fact the basis of true 'thought', while 'thought' is, in fact, the activity of real suchness. The real suchness of self-nature is what evolves 'thought', for the eyes, nose, ears, and tongue themselves cannot think. The real suchness is of such nature that it can evolve 'thought'; should it be absent, sight and hearing, color and sound, would instantly disappear. When the real suchness of the self-nature evolves 'thought' there is seeing, hearing, awareness and knowledge through the six sense organs but without being discolored, or distorted, by the ten thousand circumstances, because the true self-nature is always serene. Thus, the sutra says, 'The capability of making a proper discrimination between all formal differences is to be in the highest reality without deviation.'" [6]

FOOTNOTES

1   Samadhi, 定 , equanimity, imperturbability. This is not to be construed as being entirely without feelings or emotions and to be immobile in the face of another's distress. Rather, this equanimity has the sense of being in balance regardless of what the turmoil may be.

It is the imperturbability of an efficient physician in time of critical emergency. The emotions of mercy and compassion are not absent but they became goads to greater constructive activity rather than to weeping, wailing and caterwauling.

2 Four perspectives, 四相 , avastha, or the four relations.
我相 ; 不可自私和自利 : The perspective of self---one must not be selfish or self-seeking.
人相 ; perspective of others, 除痛癢無關 , discard the attitude that sufferings of others is of no concern.
眾生相 ; perspective of humanity, 斷除範圍 , 分形絶界 , break and remove all barriers so as not to separate any other human being, regardless of color, creed or nationality from one's concern.
壽者相 ; perspective of self in future, 明暸修道 無求無得 , one must understand that in the practice of Buddhism, there is neither seeking nor attaining, i.e. there is nothing to be sought as a goal or reward, so there is no such attainment.

3 From the Vimalakirti Sutra, Chapter IV, On the Bodhisattvas, 淨明經菩薩品第四 直心是道場 直心是淨土 .

4 Sariputra 舍利弗
One of the ten principal disciples of the Buddha. He was born at Nalandagrama, the son of Sarika and Tisya. He was noted for his wisdom and learning and figures prominently in certain sutras.
In the Vimalakirti Sutra, Chapter of the Disciples (III), 淨明經 , 弟子品 第三 , he was reproved by Vimalakirti for thinking that one has to sit in a certain posture, in a certain place and to be not thinking of a thing before one can be considered to be practicing dhyana. Vimalakirti explained the errors of Sariputra's conceptions to him.

5 If you do not understand the meaning of the Dharma and are yourself in error, this is understandable, but what of its effects upon others! 若不識法意 , 自錯猶可 , 更勸他人 . That is, one must be very careful in interpreting the Dharma, otherwise, the guilt of leading others toward an erroneous path will also be ours.

6 'The capability of making a proper discrimination between all formal differences is to be in the highest reality without deviation', from Vimalakirti Sutra, Chapter I.
淨明經 佛國品第一 能善分別諸法相 於第一義而不動

CHAPTER V

THE PROFOUND PRACTICE
坐禅品

The Master said to the gathering, "This doctrine of sitting in meditation is not fundamentally to concentrate upon the mind; nor is it to concentrate upon stillness, nor yet upon imperturbability. If anyone says that it is to concentrate upon the mind, he should know that the mind is fundamentally unreal. Realizing that the mind is like a mirage, it will follow that there is nothing upon which to concentrate!

"If anyone speaks of concentrating on stillness, he should know that the nature of man is originally quiet. It is because of deluded thoughts that the real suchness is concealed. But if there are no deluded thoughts our nature becomes clear and quiet of itself. If you start concentrating the mind on stillness, you will merely produce an unreal stillness. Since unreality itself has no locale, concentrating itself becomes unreal. Quiescence itself has neither shape nor form. Just to create a formalized stillness and to say that this is the thing, is to take a view that bars yourself from your own self-nature. It is indeed to be bound by the knot of stillness.

"Virtuous and learned counselors, to practice imperturbability you have only at all times to regard people as people without noticing their rights and wrongs, virtues and vices, errors and disadvantages. This is already the imperturbability of self-nature. A deluded person concentrates on the immobility of the body, but as soon as he

65

opens his mouth, he talks of other peoples' rights and wrongs, successes and failures, good and evil, and how these people disregard and violate the Dharma. Thus, if you concentrate the mind to fix it upon quiescence, you are certainly obstructing yourself from the Dharma.

The Master said further to the assembly, "What does the term meditation mean? In this school it means a mind without barriers, without obstacles. The absence of biased thoughts towards all situations and incidents is called 'sitting'. The dhyana means to realize within ourselves the imperturbability of self-nature.

"Virtuous and learned counselors, what is the meaning of the terms dhyana and equanimity? Dhyana is to be detached from all external forms. Equanimity is the complete absence of confusion within. To be attached to external forms is immediately to be confused within one's mind. But if you are detached from external forms, the mind is at once unconfused. The original nature of itself becomes quiet and of itself attains equanimity.

"You become confused only because you mull over situations when you meet with them, but if you can meet all situations and your mind is unconfused (unattached), this is true equanimity. To have dhyana towards things external, and equanimity towards things internal, is the meaning of tranquil-equanimity.

"The Bodhisattva Sila Sutra says, 'Our self-nature is at root clear and quiet. In every succeeding thought you should realize the clarity and quiescence of your self-nature. By cultivating and practicing this for yourself, you yourself will attain Buddhahood.'"

CHAPTER VI

REPENTANCE-RESOLUTION
懺悔品

Seeing at that time that scholars and laymen from Kwang Chou, Shao Chou, and the surrounding areas had gathered together in the mountain to hear the Dharma, the Great Master took his seat and addressed them saying, "Draw near, all of you, what we are concerned with here must arise from within our self-nature. At all times as thought follows thought, one's mind must be naturally quiet. By cultivating and practicing this for yourselves, you may realize your own Dharmabody, and realize that your mind is Buddha. It is only by delivering and disciplining yourselves that your coming here will not be in vain. Since you have come here from so far, our meeting at this place implies a karmic affinity.

"Now will you all kneel on one knee? First, we will talk about the self-nature, and the five fragrances of the Dharmabody. Then I will instruct you in the formless repentance." Everyone then knelt.

The Master said, "The first fragrance is discipline. This is to have one's mind thoroughly without disparagement and without evil, without envy and without greed or anger, without violence and destructiveness. This is called the fragrance of discipline.

"The second is the fragrance of equanimity. This is to behold all things good and evil, all circumstances and forms, without being confused in one's own mind. This is called the fragrance of equanimity.

"The third is the fragrance of wisdom. This is to have no obstacles in one's mind, and always to turn the light of wisdom upon one's self-nature, refraining from all evils. Though you practice all the virtues, your mind is not attached to any of them. You are respectful to superiors and considerate to inferiors, and sympathetic to the destitute and the poor. This is called the fragrance of wisdom.

"The fourth is the fragrance of detachment. This is to have no aspiration in one's mind...not to think about virtue and not to think about vice, to be serene without hindrances. This is called the fragrance of detachment.

"The fifth is the fragrance of the detachment from opinions. With the mind already without aspirations and without good or evil (attachments), one must avoid sinking into a useless cherishing of silence. (This then means that) you should study extensively and listen frequently, and realize your original mind, attaining an understanding of all the principles of Buddhism. It is to take all events in a mellow spirit without (thought of) self or others,[1] aiming directly at bodhi, whose true nature is unchanging. This is called the fragrance of the detachment from opinions. You must light the (incense of) these fragrances within yourselves. Do not seek them outside.

"Now, I am going to teach all of you the formless repentance-resolution,[2] ridding the three divisions of our life from evil, so that, all can clarify and quiet the three karmas.

"Virtuous and learned counselors, all of you say these words after me, 'I, Brother O, from now on, as my past,

68

present, and future thoughts follow one another, will not let them be discolored by ignorance and delusions. The evil karma of guilt arising from ignorance and delusions which I have accumulated from the past, I completely acknowledge and repent; and resolve to bring them instantly to an end, nevermore to arise.

'I, Brother O, from now on, as my past, present, and future thoughts follow one another, will not let them be discolored by arrogance and deceit. The evil karma of guilt arising from arrogance and deceit which I have accumulated from the past, I completely acknowledge and repent; and resolve to bring them instantly to an end, nevermore to arise.

'I, Brother O, from now on, as my past, present, and future thoughts follow one another, will not let them be discolored by attachment and jealousy. The evil karma of guilt arising from attachment and jealousy, which I have accumulated from the past, I completely acknowledge and repent; and resolve to bring them instantly to an end, nevermore to arise.'

"Virtuous and learned counselors, the foregoing is the formless repentance-resolution. What is the meaning of repentance? What is the meaning of resolution? Repentance is to repent of one's past errors from which have arisen the evil karma of guilt arising from stupidity, delusion, arrogance, deceit, attachment, and jealousy. To repent of them completely so that they never arise again, is what is meant by repentance. Resolution means that having now realized awakening, one will henceforth cut off all which brings the evil karma of guilt arising from stupidity, delusion, arrogance, deceit, attachment, and jealousy, and never repeat it. This is the meaning of resolution, so that we speak of repentance and resolution together.

69

"Ordinary people being under ignorance and delusion know only repentance of their past misdeeds; they do not know how to resolve against future errors. Because of this lack of resolution, their past guilt is not terminated and the errors will arise again in the future. If guilt from the past has not been terminated and errors arise again in the future, how can this be called repentance?

"Now that we have made this act of repentance, we should all make the four great vows. Each one of you should devote his mind to complete attention. 'We vow to deliver all beings within our own minds. We vow to cut off the limitless passions within our own minds. We vow to learn the limitless Dharma within our self-nature. We vow to attain the highest degree of Buddhahood within our self-nature.'

"Virtuous and learned counselors, if you have the great compassion, how can you not vow to deliver all beings without limit? But in so doing, it is not I, Hui Neng, that is delivering them. [3]

"The beings within the mind are those which are called the erroneous and deluded mind, the vicious mind, the deceitful and false mind, the attached and jealous mind, the evil and poisonous mind. All such types of minds are 'all beings.' Everyone must deliver them from his self-nature. This is called genuine deliverance.

"What is the meaning of self-deliverance within one's self-nature? It is to deliver warped views, passions, ignorance, grasping, and all such beings within one's mind by means of perfect view. As soon as you have perfect view, then the wisdom of bodhi, will demolish those ignorant, grasping, deluded and wishful beings. One delivers each by the appropriate means: error is delivered by or-

70

thodoxy; delusion is delivered by realization; ignorance is delivered by knowledge; evil is delivered by virture. Being delivered in this way is called genuine deliverence.

"As to the vow, to cut off limitless passions, it is to use the prajna wisdom of self-nature to eradicate empty and false thinking from the mind.

"As to the vow to study the limitless Dharma, this is the necessity to practice constantly the orthodox Dharma of seeing into one's self-nature. This is the meaning of genuine learning.

"As to the vow to attain the highest Buddhahood, this means that when you can always have your mind under the discipline of the real orthodox (Dharma), letting go of both delusions and awakening, and when you have prajna always arising, casting off both the real and the unreal... then you will see the Buddha-nature, then you will attain Buddhahood at the mere mention of the word. The way to practice these vows is to do it constantly from moment to moment.

"Now that we have made the four great vows, I will instruct you in the formless Three Refuges.[4]

"Virtuous and learned counselors, we take refuge in bodhi because it is the ultimate of both merit and prajna.

"We take refuge in perfect view because it is the ultimate of the abandoning of desires.

"We take refuge in equanimity because it is the ultimate quality even among large numbers of people.

"From this day onward, regarding bodhi as teacher, we shall no more take refuge in those erroneous views of the evil one or in those who are outside the Dharma, but (will abide) with the three gems of our self-nature whose brilliance are always self-evident.

"I advise you to take refuge in the three gems of your self-nature, in the Buddha, (which means) to be awakened; in the Dharma, which means to hold the perfect view; in the Sangha, which means equanimity. If in your own mind you take refuge in bodhi, error and delusion do not arise, desires are diminished, contentment is realized, and you are able to be detached from wealth and form. This is called the ultimate of both merit and prajna.

"If in your own mind you take refuge in perfect view, one thought follows another without false views. When there are no false views, then there is no self or others, no arrogance, greed, lust, prejudice, or attachment, and this is called the ultimate of the abandoning of desires.

"If in your own mind you take refuge in equanimity, it is to have one's self-nature uncolored by or attached to any kind of worldly anxieties, lusts, desires, and conditions. This is called the ultimate quality even among large numbers of people.

"If you practice it in this way, this is to take refuge in yourself. [5] Not understanding this, ordinary people may recite the three refuges from morning to night, but if this is taking refuge in the Buddha, where is the Buddha? If you cannot see the Buddha, in what do you trust for refuge? Such words are the height of delusion.

"Virtuous and learned counselors, everyone must look deeply into himself and not use his mind in the wrong way.

The sutras make this distinction clearly, saying to take refuge in the Buddha within oneself. They do not say to take refuge in any other Buddha. If you do not take refuge in your own Buddha, you have nowhere in which to take refuge. But now if you have realized yourself, each one of you should take refuge in the three gems of his own mind. Within, to set the nature of one's own mind in order; without, to be respectful to others; this is to take refuge within oneself.

"Now that you have already taken refuge in your own three gems, you should all pay attention, as I am going to explain the identity of the Trikaya[6] with the Buddha of the self-nature. By this means you can all see your own Trikaya and thus realize your own self-nature.

"All of you follow what I say, 'We take refuge in the clear, quiet Dharmakaya[6] Buddha of our own physical body. We take refuge in the one hundred thousand Nirmanakaya[6] Buddhas in our own physical body. We take refuge in the all embracing Sambhogakaya[6] Buddha, within our own physical body.' The physical body is the hostel (of the Trikaya) but it cannot be said to be its home, for the Trikaya Buddha is within our self-nature. All people whatsoever have it. But because your own mind is deluded, you do not see your inner nature and so seek the Trikaya Buddha externally, not realizing that the Trikaya Buddha dwells in the midst of one's own body.

"All of you listen to my teaching. It will enable you to purify your self-nature and find the Trikaya Buddha within your own bodies. This Trikaya Buddha arises from our self-nature and is not to be acquired from without.

"What is the meaning of the clear and quiet Dharmakaya Buddha? The nature of a human being is originally clear and quiet, and the ten thousand things arise from its self-nature. From thinking about the evil, there arises evil deeds. From thinking about the virtuous, there arises good deeds. It is the same with all other matters within self-nature. It is like the sky which is forever clear and where the sun and moon are always bright. Yet, because floating clouds may obscure them, then it is bright above but dark below. But suddenly the wind arises and the clouds are scattered; then it is bright both above and below, and the outlines of everything become visible. The self-nature of an ordinary being is always floating and wandering and is like the clouds in the sky.

"Virtuous and learned counselors, knowledge is like the sun, prajna like the moon, and prajna-wisdom is always shining, but the state of attachment to external circumstances allows deluded thoughts to obscure the self-nature like floating clouds, and then its brightness is not realized. However, if you encounter and listen to the true and orthodox Dharma, and you of yourselves get rid of delusions, then there will be clear understanding both within and without, so that the ten thousand things will all become visible within your self-nature. One who has realized his self-nature is indeed like this and this is called the clear and quiet Dharmakaya Buddha.

"Virtuous and learned counselors, to take refuge in the self-nature of our own mind is to take refuge in the true Buddha. One who does this completely discards from within his self-nature the non-virtuous mind, the envious and jealous mind, the fawning and flattering mind, the egotistically, selfish mind, the deceitfully, lying mind, the deprecating mind, the overbearing mind, the perverted mind, the arrogant mind, and non-virtuous mental activity of every type at all times. Always to see one's own fault and not to discuss others' good or evil is to take refuge in oneself. Always to practice humility and to maintain an attitude of universal reverence, this is to see into one's nature with clear understanding and without further stagnation or hindrance. This is to take refuge in oneself.

"What is the meaning of the ten billion fold Nirmanakaya? If one does not think of the ten thousand things, one's nature is fundamentally like the void. But one moment's pondering is called transformation. Thinking about evil matters transforms one into the purgatories. Thinking about virtuous matters transforms one into the heavens. (Thinking) maliciously transforms one into dragons and serpents. (Thinking) of mercy and compassion transforms one into a Bodhisattva. (Thinking) prajna transforms one into the transcendental world. Thinking stupidity and attachments transforms one into the inferior regions. One's self-nature has these multitudes of transformations of which the deluded person is unaware. If the succession of thoughts is evil, one is always following the evil path, but, if you return to a single virtuous thought prajna immediately arises. This is called the Nirmanakaya Buddha of self-nature.

"What is the meaning of the perfect Sambhogakaya? For example, as a lamp can remove a darkness which has existed for a thousand years, so a simple thought of wisdom can put an end to ten thousand years of stupidity. Do not think about the past, which, having gone by, cannot be grasped; nor be always thinking of the future. When each successive thought is sufficient unto itself [7] you see into your self-nature.

"Although good and evil are different, our self-nature is non-dual, and this non-dual nature is called the genuine nature. Within this genuine nature there is no coloring by virtue or vice and this is what is called the perfect

Sambhogakaya Buddha. When a single evil thought arises within our self-nature it annuls the good karma of ten thousand kalpas. But when a single virtuous thought arises within our self-nature, evil as many as the sands of the Ganges is brought to an end. This goes on directly until one reaches the supreme bodhi. To see into oneself in every thought without losing the clarity of the original mind is called the Sambhogakaya.

"Virtuous and learned counselors, when thinking arises in the Dharmakaya, this is then the Nirmanakaya Buddha. As we see into our self-nature as thought follows thought, this is the Sambhogakaya Buddha. Self-realization, self-discipline, and the merit-virtues of the self-nature--- these are one's true home. Skin and flesh are the physical body, but the physical body is a hostel; it is by no means our home. It is only necessary to realize the three bodies of your self-nature, then you will know the Buddha of your own self-nature.

"I have a poem of the formless which if you can put into practice, will allow you at the mere mention of the word to dissipate instantly the accumulated retribution and guilt of having been under delusion. The poem says:

Deluded persons discipline themselves for the
    sake of merits,
And not for the sake of the Dharma.

They are so deluded,
That they call self-discipline for merits the fol-
    lowing of the Dharma.

(While it is true) that alms-giving and charity
    bring merits without limit,

Yet the three evils[8] are still active within the
mind.

They intend to make an end of evil karma with
accumulated merits,
But in the future when fortune arrives the evil
karma is yet within.

The point is to remove the cause of guilt from
within the mind,
And for each person to repent truly within his
self-nature.

The sudden awakening of the Mahayana is genuine repentance,
And if you discard errors and follow the virtuous
way there will be no guilt.

To study the Dharma you must constantly look
deeply into your self-nature,
Then you will be identical with all the Buddhas.

Our patriarchs have handed down this direct
method,
Desiring that all by realizing their nature may
be as one.

If you want to seek the Dharmakaya in the right
way,
Discard all formal rituals and purify your mind
inwardly.

Resolutely see into yourselves without delay.
If you put it off you may come to a sudden end
and this life will be one of regret.

If you want to understand the Mahayana doctrine
    of realizing your self-nature,
Devote yourself with reverence to its seeking
    within the mind."

The Master said, "You should all take heed to discipline yourselves in this way. If at the mere mention of the word you see into your nature, even though you are a thousand miles away from me, it is just as if you were by my side; but if at the mere mention of these words you do not have the realization, then, though we stand face to face, yet it is as if we were a thousand miles apart. Of what use would it then have been for you to have come so far? Take good care of yourselves."

When the whole assembly had heard the doctrine, there were none who did not become open to realization, and cheerfully began to practice it.

FOOTNOTES

1　Without (thought of) self or others 無我無人
The special meaning conveyed here is that at this stage one does not
think of self as differentiated, or separated from others. Without
thinking about the self, 我 , then there will not be any comparison
of the self with 人 , others. Inasmuch as the broad scope of the
teachings is that others' problems and cares are as much our concern
as our own then there should no longer be any thought of self and
others as separate entities.

2　Repentance, Resolution 懺悔 , Ksamayati.
Repentance, 懺 ; Resolution, 悔 ;
In the academic sense, 懺 , is usually taken as the transliteration
of ksama and 悔 as its translation and thus both means repentance.
In colloquial usage the term in its usual combination of 懺悔 carries
the meaning of repenting for errors, or regret for one's wrongs. In
its specialized usage in Buddhism, which the Sixth Patriarch brings
out in this chapter, 懺 and 悔 carries distinctive and important
meanings of its own.
懺 is both the acknowledgement and the repentance of one's wrongs.
Acknowledgement means that a person is fully aware that he is wrong.
So we use repentance for 懺 .
As to 悔 , in Buddhism, it carries more meaning than just regret. Its
emphasis is on a heartfelt resolution never to commit these wrongs
again. As the Sixth Patriarch says unless the latter aspect is completely manifest then one is still, 愚迷 , ignorant and deluded.

3　But in so doing, it is not I, Hui Neng, that is delivering them.
恁麼道且不是惠能度 This sentence appears unrelated unless
we delve into the more profound doctrines of Buddhism. In the 金
剛經 第二十五 , the Diamond Sutra Chapter XXV, -- 實無有
眾生如來度者,"In reality there are no beings that the Buddha
has delivered". Because, to have the conception of a being and a
self that is delivering them would be the height of egotism, 我相 .
Thus Hui Neng's statement is definitely pertinent when we realize
what has gone on before in the Sutra. Incidentally, it is important
to study this Sutra from the beginning to the end, for, interestingly
enough, some of the doctrines laid down in the earlier chapters are
abolished in the later ones because one is assumed to have a greater
depth of understanding.

4　Three refuges, 三歸依 , Trisarana.
The three formulas of refuge or vows are usually expressed to the 三

實 the three Gems, i.e. 佛 to the Buddha, 法 the Dharma, 僧 the Sangha. The formulas are 歸依佛 , Buddham saranam gacchami, I take refuge in the Buddha; 歸依法 , Dharmam saranam gacchami, I take refuge in the Dharma; 歸依僧 , Sangham saranam gacchami, I take refuge in the brotherhood (monks). Compare this with the Sixth Patriarch's discussion.

5 This is to take refuge in yourself 是自歸依
Mahaparinirvana Sutra: "Be a lamp unto yourself, be a refuge unto yourself."

6 The Trikaya, 三身 , the three bodies or natures of Buddhahood. There are various other traditional explanations of this term. As abstracted from this sutra, the Sixth Patriarch explains as follows: (1) Dharmakaya, 法身 , the Dharma body, is 自性清淨見性 , the clear, quiet realization of one's self-nature. (2) The Nirmanakaya, 化身 , the transformation-body, is 千萬緣歸正而不變 , through countless incidents the self-nature remains unwaveringly virtuous without changing. (3) The Sambhogakaya, 報身 , not the reward body, but the retributive body which understands karma completely but neither obscures it nor is obscured by it. 明因果而不昧因果 .
Note carefully that the Sixth Patriarch says all these aspects are one and all within the individual, the attainment of which means the attainment of Buddhahood.

7 Sufficient unto itself 圓明
圓 , round, all-embracing, whole, perfect, complete; 明 , vidya, knowledge, enlightened, wise; so the implication of the statement would be that each thought should be perfect and enlightened unto itself.

8 Three evils, 三惡 , same as three poisons, 三毒 , i.e. 貪 , greed; 嗔 , anger; 癡 , ignorance or attachments.

CHAPTER VII

OPPORTUNITIES AND AFFINITIES
頓漸品

After the Master had received the Dharma at Huang Mei, he returned to Ts'ao Hou[1] Village at Shao Chou Province. But people did not know of him. At that time there was a Confucian scholar, Liu Chih Lioh,[2] who, on meeting the Patriarch, behaved with profound respect. Chih Lioh had an aunt who was a nun, named Wu Chin Ts'ang,[3] who was always reciting the Mahaparinirvana Sutra.[4] The Master after listening briefly to the recitation immediately understood its marvelous significance, and then began to explain it. At this, the nun took up the volume and questioned him about certain characters. The Master replied, "Indeed, I do not know the characters, but you may ask me about their meanings."

"But if you do not know the characters," said the nun, "how can you know their meanings?"

The Master replied, "The marvelous doctrines of all the Buddhas have nothing to do with the written word." Surprised at the unusual nature of this reply, the nun called to all the learned people around saying, "Here is a great scholar of the Dharma, whom you all should treat with hospitality."

There were present a great-great-grandson of the Marquis of the Wei dynasty, Ts'ao Shu Liang,[5] together with inhabitants of the village and they all came eagerly to pay him homage.

At that time, the old monastery of Pao Lin had been destroyed at the end of a war during the Sui dynasty. [6] Thereupon, they rebuilt the monastery upon its former foundations and made the Master welcome to live there. This monastery soon became known as Pao Fang ("a place of treasures").

The Master lived here for nine months and some days, but was once more pursued by an ill-disposed clique. Whereupon, he hid himself behind a nearby mountain. To escape when they set fire to the grass and trees, he hid himself by squeezing between the rocks so that he was able to avoid the flames. These rocks still bear the Master's knee marks, made when he was sitting in meditation, and the imprint of the texture of his clothing. Because of this, they are called the Pi Nan (Escaping Trouble) Rocks.

The Master then recalled the Fifth Patriarch's instructions to stay and conceal himself at Huai and Hui and so it was that he then went about incognito within these two counties.

* * *

Now there was a monk, Fa Hai, [7] a native of Ch'u Chiang in Shao Chou, who first visited the Patriarch and asked him saying, "'That which is mind, is that which is Buddha.' I wish you would condescend to explain this to me."

The Master replied, "Past thoughts do not arise, this is mind. Thus future thoughts do not have to be put to an end, this is Buddha. The making of all forms is mind; to be detached from these forms is Buddha. If I were to explain it completely, I could go on to the end of a kalpa without finishing. Listen to my poem which says:

When it is of the mind it is called prajna.
When it is of the Buddha it becomes equanimity.

When equanimity and prajna are alike present,
There is clarity and quietness in our intellect.

To gain an awakening into this doctrine,
You must practice it in your own self-nature.

Fundamentally it is not to start (any thoughts).
The virtuous way is to practice both (prajna and
    equanimity."

At these words, Fa Hai had the great realization and praised (the Dharma) with a poem saying:

This mind is actually the origin of the Buddha!
Not to realize it is to do oneself an injustice.

Now I know the relationship of equanimity and
    wisdom,
And that the practice of both brings detachment
    from all things.

*   *   *

The monk Fa Ta,[8] a native of Hung Chou,[9] had joined the order at the age of seven, and had always been observing the Saddharma Pundarika Sutra.[10] He came to pay his respects to the Patriarch, but (as he bowed) his head did not go all the way to the ground. The Patriarch rebuked him saying, "Your bow did not reach the ground. So why make any bow at all? There must be something on your mind. What manner of practice do you follow?"

The monk replied, "The Saddharma Pundarika Sutra which I have already read three thousand times!"

The Patriarch replied, "You might have read it ten thousand times, but if you had realized the sutra's meaning you would not be so bumptious, and then you could go along with me. But now you are parading this achievement and don't even realize your error. Listen to my poem which says:

> Respects are for cutting out airs and pomposities,
> So why not touch your head to the ground?
>
> While there is an ego, there is at once a fault.
> But when you forget your merits, your wealth
>   (of wisdom) is immeasurable."

The Master again asked, "What is your name?"

He replied, "I am called Fa Ta (He Who Understands the Dharma.)"

"Your name," said the Master, "may be Fa Ta, but when have you ever understood the Dharma?"

Whereupon he spoke this poem:

> You are now named Fa Ta
> And you have recited the sutra industri-
>   ously without rest.
>
> Empty recitation gets only the sounds,

But it is the understanding mind that is
   the Bodhisattva.

Because you have now an affinity (with
      me),
I am telling you this:

But have faith in the Buddhist (Dharma)
   wordlessly---
And the lotus flower will grow from your
   mouth.

When Ta had heard this poem, he repented and expressed his thanks saying, "From now on I will be humble
and respectful to everyone. I have recited the Saddharma
Pundarika Sutra but have not understood its meaning, and
there were always doubts. O Patriarch! your wisdom is so
vast and great that I wish you would condescend to explain
the sutra's inner meaning."

"Fa Ta," said the Master, "the Dharma is readily
understood. It is only your mind that does not understand.
There are no doubts in the sutra itself; the doubts are in
your own mind. Having studied this sutra, what do you
take to be its main principle?"

Ta replied, "The roots of my nature are dark and dull.
From the start I have followed only the recitation of the
words, so how should I understand the essential principle?"

"I do not read the characters," said the Master, "but
try to recite one page of the sutra, I will then give you an
explanation of it."

Whereupon, Fa Ta recited the sutra in a loud voice
until he came to the chapter of parables. At that point

the Master said, "Stop! This sutra, after all, takes as its principle the causality (hetupratyaya) of the manifestation of the Buddhas and explains it completely with parables of many kinds without redundance. Now, what about this causality? The sutra says, 'All the world-honored Buddhas are manifested on earth for one great reason only and that one great reason is---the Buddha's doctrines.' Under outward delusion ordinary people are attached to forms, and under inward delusion they are attached to voidness. If in the world of forms one can be detached from forms, and in the world of voidness one can be detached from voidness, then there are no delusions either within or without. If you realize this teaching, your mind will open in a single moment to the Buddha's doctrines.

"Buddha is bodhi of which there are four aspects:

1. Opening the knowledge of bodhi.
2. Practicing the knowledge of bodhi.
3. Realizing the knowledge of bodhi.
4. Entering the knowledge of bodhi.

"If upon hearing this, there is the opening and practicing of bodhi then you are able to realize and to enter. Thereupon, you will understand that bodhi knowledge is evident only because of your true self-nature. You must be most careful not to make a wrong interpretation of the sutra's meaning. If you watch someone else in the process of opening, practicing, realizing, and entering bodhi, and you yourself say, 'This must be Buddha's knowledge (i.e. a Buddha), I can have no part in it' --- such an interpretation blasphemes the sutras and slanders the Buddha. For if such a person were a Buddha already, he would have had a complete understanding, and so what use would there be in his going again through the process of opening, practicing, realizing, and entering bodhi?

"You that have faith in Buddha-knowledge should now know that it is only your own mind, apart from which there is no other Buddha. It is because all ordinary people with their greed and love of temporal conditions have concealed enlightenment from themselves so that external incidents disturb them inwardly. Yet they are content to be so driven. It was because of this that the World Honored One (the Buddha) was bestirred to arise from samadhi and, with all kinds of eloquence, persuade them to abandon desires and refrain from seeking externally, so that there might be no duality between themselves and the Buddha. Therefore, it is said, 'Be open to Buddha-knowledge'.

"I, too, persuade all men to be open constantly to Buddha-knowledge within their own minds. But the ordinary man's mind is distorted; in stupidity and delusion he commits evil; his talk is virtuous but his mind is vicious, greedy, angry, jealous, fawning, boasting, and egotistical; he interferes destructively with other peoples' business. (All this is) opening oneself to vulgar knowledge.

"But if you can perfect the mind; if you can constantly grow in wisdom; if you can turn your own light inwards upon your own mind; if you can cease from evil and practice virtue; this is to open yourself to Buddha-knowledge. You should open yourself to Buddha-knowledge at every moment, but not to vulgar knowledge. To be open to Buddha-knowledge is precisely to be out of this world (of changes), but to be open to vulgar knowledge is precisely to be in the world (of changes). But, if all that you do is to make a busy recitation (of the sutras), treating it as a chore, how do you differ from a yak chasing his tail?"

Ta then asked, "If this be true, then it is only necessary to get the understanding and not necessary to recite the sutras. Is that right?"

The Master replied, "What is wrong with the sutras and what is there to prevent your reciting them? Delusion or realization depends only upon the individual, and thus the harm or gain (from recitation) depends on yourself. To recite with the mouth and also to practice with the mind is truly to revolve the sutra. But to recite it with your mouth without practicing it in your mind is to be revolved by the sutra. Listen to my poem which says:

When the mind is deluded the Saddharma Punda-
    rika rotates us,
But the awakened mind rotates the Saddharma.

To recite the sutra for a long time without under-
    standing,
Is to be in conflict with its meaning.

The proper way is to recite it without motive
    (i.e. without seeking merit);
When there is motive the recitation is complete-
    ly distorted.

But whether you have a motive or not, whatever
    you do, don't count [11]
And then you will always be riding in the cart
    of the white bullock." [12]

While Ta was listening to this poem, his eyes had un-knowingly moistened with regret, but at these words he had the great awakening. Thereupon, he said to the Master, "Until this moment Fa Ta had not really absorbed the Saddharma Pundarika, but rather had been absorbed by it."

He asked again saying, "The sutra says all maha sravakas including even the Boddhisattvas, though they exhaust themselves in cogitating and evaluating, cannot fathom Buddha-knowledge. Now, you allow that an ordinary person has only to realize his own mind and this may then be called Buddha-knowledge. If one were not of superior intelligence this might lead to doubt and blasphemy. Furthermore, the sutra speaks of three carts: the goat's, the deer's and the white ox's. How are they distinguished? I wish you would condescend to explain this further to me."

"The sutra's meaning," replied the Master, "is quite clear, but it is you who are deluded and backward. The reason why members of the three vehicles cannot fathom the Buddha-knowledge is because of their error in trying to evaluate. However much one may exhaust oneself in thinking and pondering, this only turns him further away from (the truth). Fundamentally, the Buddha spoke only because there are ordinary people, and not because of the Buddhas. If there are those unwilling to have faith in this principle, let them withdraw from this gathering. Who would have thought that one already in the white bullock cart should still be outside looking for the three carts! Furthermore, the sutra clearly explains to you that there is only one vehicle of Buddhism. There are really no other vehicles, such as a second or a third. However, there are countless numbers of expedients of teaching and various kinds of affinitive incidents, examples, illustrations, and discussions. Therefore, this method involves only one vehicle of Buddhism.

"Why don't you wake up to the fact that the three carts are an expediency required by the needs of olden times? The truth is that there is but one vehicle and this is what is required for today. I want only to teach you to forego the expediency and to return to the truth. When you have returned to the truth (you will see also that) the truth is nameless. You should realize that this treasure belongs to you entirely and it depends on you to use it. So do not treat it as the father's idea or as the children's idea nor yet make use of any idea. This is called observing the Saddharma Pundarika Sutra. Then from one kalpa to another, your hand will not stray from the scripture and there will be no time when you are not reciting the sutra!"

Thus instructed, Ta was filled with enthusiasm and sighing happily spoke this poem of praise:

> I have read this Sutra three thousand times,
> But at one sentence from Ts'ao Ch'i, (the counting) is forgotten.

> If one does not understand the principle (of why Buddhas) are manifested,
> How can one bring to an end the vagaries of many lives.

> The three carts are but an expediency,
> And their gradations have been excellently explained.
> But who would have known that within the burning house there is the Dharmaraja. [13]

"From now on," said the Master, "one can really call you the 'Sutra-reciting Monk.'"

From thenceforth, Ta understood the profound principle and yet did not cease to recite the sutra.

*   *   *

There was a monk, Chih T'ung (智通), a native of An Feng[14] of Shu Chou[15] Province, who from the beginning (of his monastic life) had read the Lankavatara Sutra somewhat more than a thousand times and yet had not understood the Trikaya and the four wisdoms.[16] He respectfully sought the Master to explain their meanings.

"As to the Trikaya," said the Master, "the clear and quiet Dharmakaya is your very nature. The perfect fullness of the Sambhogakaya is your very knowledge. The innumerable Nirmanakaya is your very actions. If you speak of the Trikaya as something apart from your original nature, this is called having the Bodies without wisdom. If you realize that the Trikaya themselves have no self-nature, this is called the four wisdoms of bodhi. Listen to my poem:

> Self-nature already has the Trikaya and when
>   it is clearly developed the four wisdoms
>   are perfected.
>
> It is not by cutting off the objects of seeing
>   and hearing that one thereby ascends to
>   the Buddha-realm.
>
> Mark my words!
> Make up your mind firmly and have faith and
>   you will be forever without delusion.
>
> Do not copy those who seek it externally,
> Chatting all day about bodhi."

T'ung asked again, "May I hear something about the meaning of the four wisdoms also?"

"Now that you understand the Trikaya," said the

91

Master, "you should naturally understand the four wisdoms. So why ask again? If we discuss the four wisdoms apart from the Trikaya, this would be called 'wisdom without Bodies'. This would be to have wisdom and yet to return to being without wisdom."

He spoke another poem saying:

The great-round-mirror-wisdom[17] is by nature clear and quiet.
The even-natured-wisdom is the mind without sickness.[18]

The marvelous-discerning-wisdom sees without thought of merit.
The action-perfecting-wisdom is like the round-mirror-wisdom.

When the fifth, eighth, sixth, and seventh[19] ripen, transformation is effected.
But this is really a matter of words and not of reality.

If at your present state of development you do not hold back,
You will flourish and abide forever in the supreme-tranquility.

"What I have described above is the change of consciousness (識 vijnana) into wisdom (智 jnana). It says in the teaching that one first transforms the five senses (vijnanas)[19] into the action-perfecting-wisdom. The sixth intellect, (manas 意), is then changed into the marvelous-discerning-wisdom. The seventh, mano-vijnana, is then changed to the even-natured-wisdom. Then the eighth, alayavijnana, is changed to the great-round-

92

mirror-wisdom. Though manas (sixth) and mano-vijnana (seventh) contain the cause of transformation, the five senses and alayavijnana (eighth) bear fruit upon this change; but this is only a change of their names and not of their real nature (體)."

T'ung instantly realized the wisdoms of his nature and thereupon presented a poem saying:

The Trikaya is actually my own real nature,
And the four wisdoms are the enlightenment
   of the original mind.

When the Trikaya and the four wisdoms fuse
   without obstruction,
Then one responds to all things regardless of
   their forms.

To resort to methods is an entirely erroneous
   activity.
And to cherish them is not the real, genuine
   principle.

This marvelous insight arises from your (the
   Sixth Patriarch's) knowledge.
Now at last I can forget these impure names.

*　　*　　*

There was a monk, Chih Ch'ang (智常), a native of Kuei Ch'i[20] of Hsin Chou Province,[21] who had joined the order when he was very young. He was seeking determinedly to see into his own nature and came one day to pay his respects. The Master asked him saying, "Where do you come from? And what is it that you seek?"

He replied, "I have recently paid my respects to Ta Tung (大通), the monk at Pe Feng [22] Mountain at Hung Chou. From him I got the idea of seeing into one's own nature and attaining Buddhahood, but I have not yet resolved my doubts. I have come a great distance to pay my respects and humbly entreat you to point out the right direction to me."

"Try to recall," said the Master, "what he said to you."

"I was with him for more than three months without receiving any instructions. Because I had urgent reason to seek the Dharma, I went alone one night into his bedroom and respectfully asked, 'What is one's original mind and original nature?' T'ung then replied, 'Do you see the void?'"

"Yes," I answered.

"'Do you see,'" said he, "'whether the void has form or features?'"

"The void," I replied, "has no shape so how can it have form and features?"

"'Your original nature,'" he said, "'is just like the void. To understand that there is not one thing to be seen is the right view, and that there is not one thing to be known is true knowledge. It is neither green nor yellow, long nor short. Only see into the original source which is clear and quiet and there is the very substance of bodhi, perfect and luminous. This is called seeing into one's own nature and attaining Buddhahood. This is also called the

94

Tathagata jnana.[23]

"Though I have heard these words, I do not definitely understand them. I beseech you to begin to instruct me."

The Master replied, "What your master has told you still retains seeing and knowing. This accounts for your not yet understanding. I shall now point it out to you with a poem:

Not to see anything but to retain 'non-seeing',
Is much like floating clouds that cover the sun's
    face.

Not to know anything but to cherish 'not-
    knowing',
Is like a flash of lightning piercing the great
    sky.

These notions insinuate themselves in the twin-
    kling of an eye;
If you make the mistake of accepting them,
When have you really understood the meaning
    of expediency (upaya)?

In each thought you should automatically know
    when it is erroneous.
Then your inward light will always be manifest."

When Ch'ang had heard the poem, his mind was opened widely. He then offered (his own) poem saying:

To start up irrelevant conceptions,
Is to be attached to forms in seeking bodhi.

To entertain a single thought of realization,

Is no different from being in the first stages
    of delusion.

(To think that) one's nature is aware of its
    original body,
Is to follow fruitlessly an aimless light.

If I had not entered the Master's room,
I would still be confusedly chasing the two
    shadows.[24]

        *   *   *

One day Chih Ch'ang asked the Master, "The Buddha spoke of the three vehicles of the Dharma, but he also spoke of the supreme vehicle. I do not yet understand this, and I wish you would instruct me."

The Master replied, "You should concentrate on your own mind and not be attached to outward forms of doctrine. The Dharma is not (divided) into four vehicles; but peoples' minds have many classes and divisions.

"Just to attend and to listen to the exposition of the Sutras is the little vehicle. To realize the Dharma and to understand its meaning is the middle vehicle. To discipline oneself in accordance with the Dharma is the great vehicle. To understand completely all methods and to have them entirely at hand; not to be attached to anything; to cut off all forms and methods; and not (to feel) the attainment of a single thing is called the supreme vehicle. (The nature of) the vehicle is a matter of practicing the meaning and not of verbal discussions. You must practice it yourself---so do not ask me. At all times let your self-nature be naturally (in a state of) suchness."

Out of gratitude, Ch'ang became the Master's attendant for the rest of his life.

* * *

There was a monk Chih Tao (志道), a native of Nan Hai County in Kwangtung, who paid his respects to the Master and said, "Since I have joined the order, I have read the Maha Parinirvana Sutra for more than ten years, but I do not yet understand its main principles. I wish you would condescend to explain them to me."

"What part of it do you not understand?" asked the Master.

"'All deeds are impermanent is the doctrine of arising and ceasing. When arising and ceasing have ceased there is the joy of tranquil cessation.'[25] This is the part on which I have doubts."

"For what reasons," asked the Master, "do you have doubts?"

He answered, "All human beings have two bodies which are called the physical body[26] and the Dharma body. The physical body is impermanent, arising and ceasing. The Dharma body is permanent, without knowledge or awareness. When the sutra says, 'When arising and ceasing have ceased there is the joy of tranquil cessation', I do not know which body tranquilly ceases and which body is joyful. If it is the physical body, at the time when the physical body comes to an end, its four

97

elements[27] are dispersed, and this is certainly suffering, and suffering cannot be said to be joy.

"If the Dharma body is in tranquil cessation, then it is the same as straw and broken tiles---who then is the enjoyer? Furthermore, the Dharma-nature is the basis of arising and ceasing, and the five skandhas are the operation of arising and ceasing, for there is one basis and five functions. Now, arising and ceasing is perpetual; arising is when an operation emerges from the basis, cessation is when an operation is absorbed back into the basis. If one waits for it to arise again, this is to be in the class of sentient beings (and this is) not to have ended, not to have ceased. However, if one does not wait for it to arise again, then one is always in a state of tranquil cessation, which is to be the same as an insentient thing. But, if this is the case, nirvana will be the complete suppression of all things whatsoever, so that they are not able to arise, and then what joy can there be?"

The Master replied, "You are a disciple of Sakyamuni. Why be like those who do not follow the way, and who, adhering to erroneous views of annihilation and permanence, criticize the doctrine of the Supreme Vehicle? According to what you have said, the Dharmakaya is apart from the physical body and has to be detached from arising and ceasing to seek for tranquil cessation. Furthermore, in saying that nirvana is a state of permanent joy, you inferred that there is someone enjoying it. This is to be attached to the cravings of birth and death and to delight in the pleasures of illusions.

"By now, you should have realized that the Buddha (spoke) for the sake of all those deluded people who consider the union of the five skandhas to be the substantial form of a self. These people discriminate between all

98

things as external forms of matter. They crave life and fear death. They wander in their thoughts not realizing that these are but dreams and fantasies, and that they are empty and unreal. They submit themselves unnecessarily to the wheel of becoming (bhavacakra).[28] They pervert the permanent joy of nirvana into a form of suffering. Yet, they gallop around seeking it all the time.

"Because of pity for such people, the Buddha manifested the true joy of nirvana in which instantaneously there is no perspective of arising, and, also instantaneously there is no perspective of ceasing. Moreover, there is no process of (arising and ceasing) to be brought to an end. Just this, is the manifestation of tranquil cessation. Though it is manifested, yet there is no concept that it is being manifested and this is its constant joy. Of this joy there is neither a recipient nor a non-recipient, so how can there be talk of the 'one basis and the five skandhas', and how much more beside the point is it to talk of nirvana as the suppression of all things so that they never again arise? This is but blaspheming the Buddha and slandering the Dharma. Listen to my poem which says:

> The peerless great nirvana
> Is all-inclusive and its brightness shines
>   ever serenely.
>
> The vulgar and ignorant call it death;
> The uninitiated fasten on it as extinction.
>
> All those seekers of the second vehicle
> Regard it as a state of inactivity.
>
> All these views belong entirely to emo-
>   tional formulations
> And are the basis of the sixty-two erron-

eous views.[29]

These absurd formulations of empty and
    false names,
How can they be the genuine and real
    meanings?

But a person of immeasurable wisdom
Thoroughly understands that there is noth-
    ing either to be grasped or to be
    given up.

He knows of the function of the five
    skandhas
And of the ego in its midst,
Of the external manifestation of all phys-
    ical shapes
And of each and every type of tone and
    sound,
That they are all equally like dreams and
    phantasies.

Neither does he introduce the idea of
    common people and sages,
Nor does he make a concept of nirvana.
Because he has cut off the two sides[30] and
    the three periods of time.[31]

He always responds with the operation of
    all the senses,
But does not call to mind an idea of their
    operation.

He discriminates in all matters,
But does not call to mind the idea of dis-
    crimination.

Even when the fires at the end of a kalpa
    burn to the depths of an ocean,
Or when the blasting winds crash moun-
    tains together,
Yet the truly enduring joy of tranquil
    cessation
And nirvana is of the nature of unchang-
    ing suchness.

I have now spoken so emphatically
In order that you may abandon erroneous
    views.

So long as you do not follow the mere
    words,
It will enable you to understand a small
    part of it (nirvana)."

Chih Tao having heard this poem entered into a state
of profound realization, and having paid his heartfelt respects, withdrew.

*   *   *

There was a Ch'an teacher by the name of Hsing Ssu, [32]
surname Liu, who was born in An Ch'eng [33] in the province
of Chi. [34]   Having heard of the widespread meetings that
were held for the teaching of the Dharma at Ts'ao Ch'i,
he came at once to pay his respects.   At this time he
asked, "How should one apply oneself so as not to be
caught in categories?" [35]

The Master replied, "What has been your previous
practice?"

He answered, "I have not even had anything to do with the eternal truths."

"Then in what category are you?" asked the Master.

"If I have not even had anything to do with the eternal truths," he answered, "what categorization can there be?"

The Master received this answer with profound regard and let Ssu be the head of a group (of disciples).

One day the Master said to him, "You should go off and be the teacher of a separate region, for one must not let (the Dharma) break off and come to an end. Having attained the Dharma, Ssu then returned to the Ch'ing Yuan Mountains in Chi Chou and persevered in teaching with energy and regularity. He was known posthumously as the Pristine Dharma Master Hung Chi (弘濟 energetic and benevolent).

*　　　*　　　*

There was a Pristine Dharma Master, Huai Jang, [36] surnamed Tu (杜), from Chin Province (金州). He first visited the National Teacher, Hui An, [37] at Mount Sung, [38] and An sent him to pay his respects at Ts'ao Ch'i. Jang went and did so.

"Where have you come from?" asked the Master.

"From Mt. Sung," he replied.

"What thing is it that thus comes?" asked the Master.

He answered, "To speak of it as a thing is not to the point."

"Is it possible to attain it by discipline?" asked the Master.

He answered, "It is not impossible to attain it by discipline, but it is impossible to be tainted with dirt."

"It is just this 'not-being-tainted-with-dirt,'" said the Master, "which is cherished by all the Buddhas. You have already attained this and I likewise."

This immediately opened Jang's mind to a wider understanding, wherefore he became the Master's personal attendant for fifteen years and daily attained profounder understanding. He dwelt afterwards in the Nan Mountains,[39] and became a great exponent of the Pristine Dharma School. Then by imperial edict he was given the posthumous title of the Pristine Dharma Master (大慧 the great wisdom), Ta Hui.

*   *   *

The Pristine Dharma Master Hsuan Chueh[40] came from Yung Chia[41] in Wen Province[42] and was surnamed Tai (戴). In his youth he had studied the sutras and commentaries and was adept in the contemplation practices and the doctrines of the T'ien T'ai School.[43] As a result of seeing the Vimalakirti Sutra, he began to clarify his own mind. He had a meeting with the Master's disciple, Hsuan T'se,[44] who had come to see him, and together they had a pleasant conversation. The words which Hsuan Chueh spoke happened to agree (with the tradition) of all the patriarchs. T'se said, "Under what Master did you attain the Dharma?"

He replied, "I have studied all the sutras and commentaries, each one with a master's approval. Lately, in the study of the Vimalakirti Sutra, I have attained a realization of the Buddha-mind doctrine but do not have anyone to confirm me."

T'se said, "Such a thing was possible before the time of the Wei Yin Wang Buddha[45] (Bhis-ma-garjita-ghosa-svara-raja), but after this time, all those who have self realization without a master are naturally considered to be outside the way."

Chueh replied, "I wish that you would be my confirmer."

"My word," said T'se, "is of little weight, but at Ts'ao Ch'i there is the Sixth Patriarch who is a great master. People gather to him like clouds from the four directions to receive the Dharma. If you will go there I will accompany you." Therefore, Chueh went together with T'se to visit the Patriarch.

(On arriving) Chueh paid his respects to the Master three times, shook his staff, but remained standing.

"A sramana[46] of the order", said the Master, "is supposed to be completely versed in the three thousand forms of dignified conduct[47] and the eighty thousand rules of deportment.[48] Whence, O Exalted One, have you come with such great egotism?"

"Birth and death," replied Chueh, "is a serious matter. (The demon of) impermanence comes in an instant."

The Master answered, "Why not understand the essential principle of no-birth so as to make an end of swift impermanence?"

Chueh replied, "What is essential is precisely not born, and once understood swift impermanence already has come to an end."

"That is so, that is so," said the Master.

Thereupon, Hsuan Chueh made the complete ceremonial respects and proceeded at once to take his leave.

"Aren't you going away too soon?" asked the Master.

Chueh replied, "Since originally there is no such thing as motion, so how, pray, can there be quickness?"

"Who knows there is no motion?" asked the Master.

Chueh replied, "You, yourself, made the distinction, sir."

"You," said the Master, "have attained a most profound idea of no-birth."

"How," countered Chueh, "can no-birth have an idea?"

"Without an idea," returned the Master, "who then makes the distinction?"

"There can be a distinction," said Chueh, "which is not a conception."

"You have spoken well," said the Master. "At least

stay over one night."

From that time, he was called One Night Chueh. Afterwards, he wrote the Ch'eng Tao K'e [49] which was widely circulated. He was posthumously called the Great Master, Wu Hsiang (無相 , formless). Contemporarily, he was called Chen Chueh (真覺 , genuine awareness).

*   *   *

When the Pristine Dharma Master Chih Huang [50] first visited the Fifth Patriarch, he had stated that he had a complete grasp of the state of samadhi. For a long time he had been living at a small temple and had been sitting in meditation for twenty years.

When the Master's disciple, Hsuan T'se, was traveling beyond the north of the Yellow River, he heard of Huang's name and went to the small temple asking, "What are you doing here?"

"Entering into samadhi," replied Huang.

"You say you are entering into samadhi," said T'se, "are you entering intentionally, or unintentionally? If you are entering it unintentionally, then all insentient beings, grass, trees, pottery, and rocks should all attain samadhi. If you are entering it intentionally, then all those sentient beings that have consciousness should likewise attain samadhi."

"At the time I enter samadhi," replied Huang, "I do not know whether it is with or without intention."

106

"If you do not know whether it is with or without intention," said T'se, "it must be a permanent samadhi, so how can there be any leaving or entering it? If there is any leaving or entering, it is not the great samadhi."

Unable to answer, Huang thought for a while and then asked, "To which succession does your Master belong?"

"My Master," replied T'se, "is the Sixth Patriarch at Ts'ao Ch'i."

"What is the Sixth Patriarch's dhyana and samadhi?" asked Huang.

T'se answered, "According to my Master's teaching, there is a marvelous profundity[51] (of our nature) which is perfectly tranquil; basically and in function it is (in a state of) pure suchness. The five skandhas are essentially void. The six senses do not hold. There is neither leaving nor entering. There is neither peace nor confusion. The nature of dhyana is 'non-abiding' and upon the detachment of abiding, there is the tranquility of dhyana. The nature of dhyana is 'non-arising', so do not have any idea of 'arising' in dhyana or of dhyana itself. The mind is like the empty void yet there is no consideration of empty voidness."

Upon hearing these words, Huang came at once to visit the Master. The Master asked him saying, "Sir, where do you come from?"

Huang related all that had been described above, and the Master said, "It is indeed just as you have spoken."

Taking pity on him for his long journey, the Master

thereupon discussed frankly and decisively (his remaining doubts). Whereupon, Huang attained the great awakening, and the way in which he had previously trained his mind for twenty years disappeared without shadow or sound.

That evening the inhabitants of the country north of the (Yellow) river heard a voice in the sky saying, "Pristine Dharma Master Huang today attained the Dharma."

Thereafter, Huang respectfully took his leave and returned again to the country north of the river and there began to teach the four classes.[52]

*　　　*　　　*

There was a boy from Siang Yang[53] Village, named Kao Shen Hui[54] aged thirteen. He came from Yu Ch'uan Monastery[55] to pay his respects.

"You have come a long and difficult way," said the Master, "but do you come as one who has grasped the fundamentals? If you have the fundamentals, then you are the Master of your mind. Try and say something so that I can see your understanding."

He replied, "I take 'non-abiding' as fundamental; that which sees is precisely the master of the mind."

"This young disciple," said the Master, "is fit for further instruction."

Hui then asked, "Sir, when you are practicing meditation do you still see or not see?"

The Master tapped him three times with his staff saying, "When I tap you, does it hurt or not?"

"It hurts and it doesn't hurt," he replied.

"I, too," said the Master, "see and not see."

"What is it like," asked Shen Hui, "to be seeing and not seeing?"

The Master replied, "As for what I see, this is to be constantly aware of the errors and faults in my own mind. What I do not see is the right and wrong and the good and evil of other people. This is what it means to be both seeing and not seeing.

"What did you mean by saying that it both hurts and doesn't hurt? If you are not hurt, then you are like wood and stone. But if it hurts, then you are just the same as an ordinary person and would begin to be angry and aggrieved. At your stage of progress, to see and not to see is still a dualism; to hurt and not to hurt is still a matter of arising and ceasing. You have not yet even realized your own self-nature, so how do you presume to teach people?"

Shen Hui respectfully apologized and thanked the Master.

The Master continued, "If your mind is deluded and has no insight, you should ask a learned counselor so that you can find the way. If you have realized your own mind, then you can see into your self-nature by yourself and conduct yourself in accordance with the Dharma. But even though you are under delusion and are unable to see into your own mind, yet you come and ask whether I have or have not the realization.

"If I have realized (my own self-nature), I know it for myself. How could I be deluded by you? If you have realized it for yourself, neither would I be able to delude you. Why don't you know for yourself and see into your self-nature for yourself rather than to ask me whether I have the realization or not?"

Shen Hui made obeisance repeatedly---more than a hundred times, seeking pardon for his errors and faults. He became a devoted and industrious attendant who never left his master's side.

*   *   *

One day the Master addressed the assembly saying, "I have something which has neither head nor tail, neither name nor term, neither back nor front. Does anyone know what it is?"

Shen Hui started up saying, "It is the original source of all the Buddhas and also the Buddha-nature of Shen Hui."

The Master replied, "I was talking to you about a thing that has neither name nor term, and right away you call it the original source of all Buddha-nature. You must have a straw mat over your head! [56] You are one of those who have an entirely conceptual understanding.

"What I was actually talking about is the genuine original self-nature in which the true void has no substance. So where can the dust cling?"

110

After the death of the Patriarch, Hui went to Lo Yang[57] and energetically propagated the sudden doctrine of Ts'ao Ch'i. He also wrote the Hsien Tsung Chi (顯宗記 the Treatise on Manifesting the Doctrine) which was widely circulated. He was subsequently known as the Pristine Dharma Master Ho Che (荷澤).

*　　*　　*

A monk asked the Master, "Who has received the essential principles of Huang Mei (i.e. of the Fifth Patriarch)?"

The Master replied, "The person who understands Buddhism has received it."

"Have you then received it?" asked the monk.

"I," said the Master, "do not understand Buddhism."

*　　*　　*

One day the Master wanted to wash the robe which he had received, but could find no suitable stream. For this reason, he went about five li[58] behind the monastery and there beheld a thick and luxuriant mountain forest where a fresh breeze was playing. Shaking his staff, the Master struck the ground. A fountain came forth at his touch and welled up into a pool. Thereupon, he knelt down and cleansed the garment upon a rock.

There was a monk, Fang P'ien,[59] from the Western

111

part of Szechwan, who came to visit the Master.

"Venerable Sir," asked the Master, "what is your occupation?"

He replied, "I am skilled in making clay models."

"Will you try," requested the Master politely, "making a model for me to see?"

P'ien was temporarily at a loss but after several days modeled a lifelike figure (of the Patriarch) about seven inches high in a most elegant and subtle form.

"You are skilled in model-nature," chuckled the Master, "but you do not understand Buddha-nature." Thereupon, he gently palmed the top of his head in blessing, saying, "Always provide a field of merits for mankind and heaven."

Furthermore, he repaid him with an offering of clothes, which P'ien took and divided into three parts. In one part he wrapped the modeled figure; the second, he kept for himself; and the third, he wrapped in palm leaves and buried in the ground.

He then made the following vow, "When at a later time this clothing is dug up, I shall be reborn as abbott of this Monastery, and will rebuild the shrine and the building."

*   *   *

There was once a monk quoting the poem of Pristine

Dharma Master Wo Lun (臥輪) saying,

> Wo Lun has skillful means
> Which enables him to cut off all
>   thoughts,
> In the face of circumstances his
>   mind is not aroused,
> And daily, monthly, bodhi grows.

Hearing him the Master said, "This poem does not show an understanding of the mind-ground. If one were to practice in this way, one would tie himself into more knots."

Therefore, he produced this poem:[60]

> Hui Neng has no skillful means;
> He does not cut off all thoughts.
> In the face of circumstances his
>   mind is often aroused,
> So how can there be a growth of
>   bodhi?

FOOTNOTES

1   Ts'ao Hou Village   曹侯村

2   Liu Chih Lioh   劉志略

3   Wu Chin Ts'ang   無盡藏

4   Mahaparinirvana Sutra   大涅槃經
大般涅槃經   translated by Fa-hsien, B.N. 118. There are various versions translated by other writers.

5   Ts'ao Shu Liang   曹叔良

6   Sui Dynasty, 隋紀 , 589 A.D. to 618 A.D., B.N. 121.

7   Fa Hai   法海
A famous disciple of the Sixth Patriarch. He is the one that recorded this sutra.

8   Fa Ta   法達

9   Hung Chou   洪州
A district of Kiangsi Province   江西南昌縣

10   Saddharma Pundarika Sutra   法華經
法華經   or   妙法蓮華經
The wonderful truth as found in the Lotus Sutra, the one Vehicle Sutra; which is said to contain 實法 Buddha's complete truth as compared with his previous 權法 or 方便法 , i.e. partial or expedient teaching, but both are included in this perfect truth. The sutra is the Saddharma Pundarika 正法華經 or (添品)妙法蓮華經 , also known as 薩曇芬陀利經 , of which several translations in whole or part were made from the Sanskrit into the Chinese, the most popular being by Kumarajiva.

11   Don't count   不計
This is a fundamental principle in Buddhism---never to count, neither to count the deeds one has done, the experiences, nor the years. Counting puts restraints on one's development and attainment. In this particular passage it is not to count the number of times one has recited this or any other sutra. The counting as Fa Ta did, led him to feel that he had accomplished a great deal which, of course, was wrong. Neither in any virtuous acts nor deeds should one count,

for in the counting is implied, the meaning of 'seeking merit' which, too, is erroneous.

12 Cart of the white bullock 白牛車
This comes from the Saddharma Pundarika Sutra 蓮華經 where reference is made to the 三車 triyana, the three vehicles of deliverance. The 羊 , goat-drawn vehicle, or the 小乘 , small vehicle
or the 聲聞 , Sravaka class, the hearers or the obedient disciple
group. The 鹿 or 中乘 , the deer-drawn or middle vehicle or
pratyeka-Buddha, the enlightenment for self group, 緣覺 .
Then the 白牛 or 大乘 , the white bullock-drawn vehicle or Mahayana, which has the salvation of all in mind.
These three vehicles, the Buddha has said, are but expedients in
teaching, suitable to the capacity of the disciples. After all there
is only 一佛乘 , one Buddha vehicle.

13 Dharmaraja 法中王
King of the Dharma, the highest principles of the doctrine, the rep-
resentation of the Buddha in the Saddharma Pundarika Sutra.

14 An Feng 安豐
See Footnote 15.

15 Shu Chou, 壽州 ; An Feng, 安豐
Shu Chou, now Shu County of the State of An Hui. An Feng is now
southeast of Shu Chou, but formerly was part of it.

16 Four wisdoms 四智
The four forms of wisdom of a Buddha are: (1) The great-round-
mirror-wisdom, 大圓鏡智 . (2) The even-natured-wisdom, 平
等性智 . (3) The marvelous-contemplation-wisdom, 妙觀察
智 . (4) The action-perfecting-wisdom, 成所作智 .

17 Great-round-mirror-wisdom 大圓鏡智
When the self-nature is clear and quiet it is also called the 大圓
鏡智 .

18 The-even-natured-wisdom is the mind without sickness
平等性智心無病
平等性智 , the even-natured-wisdom is like the Buddha's seeing
all things, 觀一切法 , and all beings in the same even light, 皆

115

悉平等 . Also see Chapter XVIII of Diamond Sutra.
The mind without sickness, 心無病 . In seeing all people, if towards some, there is a liking, 愛 , and towards others a disliking, 憎 , then the mind has 隔礙 , barriers and obstacles (to all mankind). To have this is to be with sickness, 有病 . Therefore, one should have no distaste in one's mind for anyone before we can be "a mind without sickness".

19 Fifth, 五 ; eighth, 八 ; sixth, 六 ; seventh, 七 .
The fifth, 五 , refers to the five senses, vijnanas 眼耳鼻舌身 seeing, hearing, smelling, tasting and touching which transforms the action-perfecting-wisdom 成所作智 .
The sixth, 六 , is the 意 manas, thought or perception, which alone transforms into the 妙觀察智 , the marvelous-discerning-wisdom.
The seventh, 七 , is the 心識 , the mind-sense, or mind-function. The seventh is also defined as the 末那識 manovijnana, which translates into 意 , in its deeper meaning as the mind, the total conscious mental activity. (See Glossary, Intellect). This includes the 意 , as the coordinator of the five senses and collectively becomes the 平等智 , the even-natured-wisdom.
The eighth, 八 , is the 阿賴耶識 , the alaya-vijnana, the mind in its conscious and unconscious aspect, the storehouse of the mind, this forms the great-round-mirror-wisdom.

20 Kuei Ch'i 貴谿

21 Hsin Chou, 信州 ; Kuei Ch'i, 貴谿 . Both are now counties in Kiangsi.

22 Pe Feng Mountain, 白峰山 , at Hung Chou, 洪州 , Kiangsi.

23 Tathagata Jnana 如來知見
Tathagata , 如來 , (a) one of the highest titles of the Buddha; (b) such as it comes.
Jnana, 知見 , to know, to know by seeing; becoming, aware, intellection; the function of knowing; views, doctrines.
So the term together means the knowledge of the Buddha.

24 Two shadows or heads 兩頭
The term refers to the poem the Sixth Patriarch gave him. The first shadow is the concept of 'non-seeing', 無見 , and the second, 守空知 , the concept of 'not-knowing'. The Master had advised him

116

not to retain either view for their retention means that one is still deluded.

25 Tranquil cessation 寂滅
The state of being unruffled, undisturbed and quietly cheerful. The complete absence of redundancy in the mind. It is cognizance without agitation. This is a practice towards liberation, but it is occasionally mistaken for nirvana itself.

26 Physical body, form body, 色身 , Rupakaya.
The flesh and blood body; as contrasted with the 法身 dharmakaya, the immaterial, spiritual, or immortal body.
Note also that the Sixth Patriarch calls this physical body 'a hostel and not home'.

27 Four elements 四大
The four elements of which all things are made i.e. earth 地 ; water 水 ; fire 火 ; and wind (or air) 風 . They represent solid 堅 ; liquid 濕 ; heat 煖 ; and motion 動 : motion produces and maintains life.

28 Bhavacakra, wheel of becoming, 輪迴 ; 輪轉 Samsara.
The turning of the wheel, to revolve, i.e. transmigration in the six ways, the wheel of transmigration; the round of existence, of life and death.

29 Sixty-two erroneous views 六十二見
三心 : The mind of the past 過去心 ; present 現在心 ; and future 未來心 .
四相 : Four avasthas or four perspectives. The perspective of self 我相 ; the perspective of others 人相 ; the perspective of humanity 眾生相 ; and the perspective of self-in-future 壽者相 .
五蘊 : Five skandhas. The five aggregates or components or attributes of a person.
十二因緣 : Twelve hetupratyayas. The twelve causative incidents or circumstantial causes of an occasion or event.
六識 : Six vijnanas or senses. The six senses are the six qualitative perceptive functions e.g. seeing, hearing, smelling, tasting, touching and ideation performed by its respective organ in response to stimuli.
六慾 : The attractive-attachments of each of the six organs.
戒 , 定 , 慧 : Sila, samadhi, prajna or discipline, equanimity,

117

wisdom.

法，妄，浮： 法 Method as in a one-track mind approach; 妄 unfounded as in day dreamings; 浮 floating as in the lack of direction in the purpose of one's life.

偏，邪，執： 偏 Slanted as to favor oneself in a report; 邪 distorted e.g. with little regard for the truth; 執 stubbornly opinionated.

住，滯，留： 住 To dwell e.g. in ideas of which one is particularly fond; 滯 stagnation e.g. to be obstructed by an incident which one cannot resolve; 留 the accumulation of irrelevant, superfluous conceptions.

迷，癡，戀： 迷 To be deluded, the misconception of everyday circumstances as being permanent; 癡 attachment to things and ideas which one knows are erroneous, but one is reluctant to give up, therefore, one rationalizes one's position with personal and colloquial views; 戀 the emotional attachment to things or ideas which are erroneous to the extent that one says, "I can't help it". "I'm born that way".

七情： The seven emotions. 喜 happiness; 怒 anger; 哀 grief; 樂 joy; 愛 love; 惡 dislike; 慾 desires.

四癡： The four attachments. 酒 Over-indulgence in alcohol; 色 over-indulgence in sex; 財 avariciousness; 氣 anger particularly as in frustrations.

30　Two sides 二邊
Being and non-being, 有無也 ; affirmation and negation, 是 , 非 ; permanence and impermanence, 常 , 無常

31　Three periods of time 三際
The past 過去 , present 現在 and the future 未來 .

32　Hsing Ssu 行思 (? - - d 740 A.D.)
A native of 安城, An Ch'eng, of 江西省 , Kiangsi Province. A disciple of the Sixth Patriarch, who later established his own monastery at the 青原 , Ch'ing Yuan Mountains of Chi Chou, called the 居淨寺 'The Tranquil Life Monastery'. He is frequently refered to as 青原行思, Ch'ing Yuan Hsing Ssu.

33　An Ch'eng 安城
A village in the Province of Kiangsi, 江西省 .

34 Chi Chou 吉州
So named in the T'ang Dynasty. Now part of Kiangsi Province, 江
西省 .

35 Categories 階級
e.g. Yanas, schools, stages of progress, as well as partial views of
the doctrine.

36 Huai Jang 懷讓
Nan Yueh Huai Jang, (678 A.D. - 775 A.D.) born 唐儀鳳二年
四月八日 April 8, 678 A.D., the youngest of three children. He
became interested in Buddhism at the age of ten and taking leave
from his parents, went to live in the 玉泉寺 , Yu Ch'uan Monastery. He became a well known disciple of the Sixth Patriarch, serving him for fifteen years.

37 National Teacher Hui An 惠安國師
National Teacher 國師 , a title conferred by the government on
eminent Buddhist scholars. Hui An 惠安 , was a native of Chih
Ch'ang 支江 , of Ching Province 荊州 . He taught for many years
at Mount Sung 嵩山 . He died in 710 A.D.

38 Mount Sung 嵩山
Six miles north of 登封縣 , Teng Feng County.

39 Nan Mountain 南嶽
Also known as 衡山 , Heng Shan, a mountain in Hunan Province
湖南 .

40 Hsuan Chueh, also written Chio, 玄覺 , (Hsuan Chueh, 665 A.D.
- 713 A.D.)
Originally a famous leader of the 天台止觀圓妙法門 , T'ien-
t'ai School of Meditation. Subsequently a disciple of the Sixth Patriarch and the author of various works, the most well-known being
the 證道歌 , Ch'eng Tao K'e. The Song of the Attainment of the
Dharma.

41 Yung Chia 永嘉
A district in Wen Province 溫州 . Now a district in 浙江 , Che
Kiang.

42 Wen Province 溫州
A name used during the T'ang Dynasty, now part of 浙江 , Che Kiang Province.

43 T'ien T'ai, 天台 , School.
A school of Buddhism founded by 陳德安 , Ch'en Te An, A.D. 538-597. It bases its tenets on the Lotus Sutra 法華經 . It maintains the identity of the Absolute and the world of phenomena and seeks to attain its secrets by meditation and contemplation.

44 Hsuan T'se 玄策
A disciple of the Sixth Patriarch, originally from 婺州 , Wu Province.

45 Wei Yin Wang, 威音王 , Bhisma-garjita-ghosa-svara-raja.
The king with the awe-inspiring voice, the name of the original Buddha appearing countless kalpas earlier. The name of the kalpa was 離衰 , Li Shuai.

46 A Sramana 沙門者
Refers to Buddhist monks who have left their families and quieted their passions. He is merciful to all, and harmful to none.

47 Three thousand forms of dignified conduct 三千威儀
(1) A term (i.e. 3,000) also used for many, a multiplicity.
(2) A monk's regulations amount to about 250; these are multiplied by four for the conditions of walking, standing, sitting, and sleeping, and thus make 1,000; again multiplied by three for past, present, and future, they become 3,000 regulations.

48 Eighty thousand rules 八萬細行
A term (80,000) used for many, beyond counting, i.e. complete, therefore all the fine details of conduct.
細 , means fine, small, minute, in detail; careful.
行 , practices, conduct, deportment.

49 Ch'eng Tao K'e 證道歌
The Song of the Attainment of the Dharma.

50 Chih Huang 智隍
A native of 河北 , Hopei Province, who originally studied under

the Fifth Patriarch. Chih Huang felt that the complete cessation of all thinking was the quintessence of Buddhism. He practiced this for twenty-four years until he was jarred out of his complacency by Hsuan T'se, a disciple of the Sixth Patriarch. Whereupon Huang also went to see the Master.

51 Marvelous profundity (of our nature) 妙湛
Refers to the 法身, the Dharmakaya, especially its formless 無相 aspect.

52 Four classes 四眾
The four varga (groups or orders) i.e. bhiksu, monks, bhiksuni, nuns, upasaka, male devotees, and upasika, female devotees. The latter two groups being those who are living with their families; the former two, in monasteries and convents.

53 Hsiang or Siang Yang 襄陽
Siang Yang Village in Hupei Province 湖北 . The birthplace of Shen Hui 神會 .

54 Kao Shen Hui 高神會 , also known as Ho-tse Shen-Hui 荷澤神會 . One of the more prominent of the Patriarch's disciples. (668 A.D. - 770 A.D.)

55 Yu Ch'uan Monastery 玉泉寺
A famous monastery in Hupei 湖北 , where Shen Hui 神會 , Huai Jang 懷讓 , Shen Hsiu 神秀 , and others have resided.

56 You must have a straw mat over your head 汝向去有箬蓋頭也
A colloquial term meaning that a person's intellect is covered up and that he blunders around like one blindfolded.

57 Lo Yang 洛陽
In the text the name used is 京 Capitol 洛 , i.e. Lo Yang the name of the ancient capitol of China beginning under the Eastern Han Dynasty 25 A.D. for over a thousand years. It is in 河南 Honan Province.

58 Five li 五里
Each 里 = 1890 feet; 五里 = 1.7 miles.

59 Fang P'ien 方辯
A native of western part of Szechwan, 四川之西 .

60 Poem
This poem is particularly for Wo Lun's 病 , sickness, i.e. the sickness of being "able to cut off all thoughts".

CHAPTER VIII

THE SUDDEN AND GRADUAL SCHOOLS

機緣品

At the time when the Patriarch was living at Ts'ao Ch'i, at the Pao Lin Monastery (in the South), Shen Hsiu the Great Master was at Ching Nan,[1] at Yu Ch'uan Monastery (in the North). Both schools were then flourishing widely. People everywhere called the Southern (school) Neng, and the Northern school Hsiu, thereby making two schools, Southern and Northern, respectively the sudden and the gradual.

Yet the students did not realize the fundamental principle of these schools (so) the Patriarch addressed the assembly saying, "Essentially, there is only one school of the Dharma, but people are of the South and of the North. There is one kind of Dharma, but the realization of it may be slow and halting. What then is the meaning of sudden and gradual? There is no (distinction between) sudden and gradual in the Dharma, but there is brilliance and dullness in people, and so we speak of sudden and gradual for this reason."

However, Shen Hsiu's disciples sometimes ridiculed the Patriarch of the Southern school saying, "He doesn't even know a single character so what claim has he to eminence?"

Shen Hsiu said, "He (i.e. Hui Neng) has attained knowledge of the deepest realization of the supreme jnana without any master. I cannot be compared to him. Fur-

123

thermore, my own Master, the Fifth Patriarch, personally transmitted the robe and the Dharma to him. Would he had done so without good cause? I regret that I am unable to go all the way to be with him personally. It is in vain that I have received honor from the nation. All of you should not remain here. Whenever you are able, go to Ts'ao Ch'i to study and decide for yourself."

One day, he commanded his disciple Chih Ch'eng,[2] saying, "You are brilliant and have much knowledge. You can go on my behalf to Ts'ao Ch'i and listen to the doctrine. If you can, retain what you hear completely in memory; come back and tell me about it."

Chih Ch'eng accepted this order and went to Ts'ao Ch'i where he joined a group that was conferring with (the Patriarch) without saying where he had come from.

Whereupon, the Patriarch spoke to the gathering saying, "There is a person hidden in this group who has come to steal the Dharma."

Chih Ch'eng at once came forth, paid his respects, and explained his business.

The Master said, "Coming from Yu Ch'uan, you should be a spy."

"It is not so," he replied.

"How can it not be so," said the Master.

"If I had not declared it, it would be so, but since I have declared it, it is not so."

The Patriarch asked, "How does your own Master

teach his followers?"

Ch'eng replied, "He is always directing and teaching all of us to concentrate on the mind and contemplate upon it until it is still, and to sit up erectly for a long time without lying down.

"To concentrate on the mind and contemplate upon it until it is still," said the Master, "is a disease and not the pristine doctrine. To restrain the body by sitting up for a long time---of what benefit is this towards the doctrine? Listen to what my poem says:

In life only to sit up and never to lie down;
In death only to lie down and never to sit up;
After all just a matter of foul bits of bones!
How can such be a basis for merits or demerits?"

Chih Ch'eng once more paid his respects saying, "I have studied the Dharma at the Great Master Hsiu's place for nine years without attaining any realization. But now upon hearing you only once, I can already understand my original mind. Birth and death is a matter of great urgency for me. May I ask you out of your great compassion, to instruct me further?"

The Master said, "I hear that your teacher instructs the students in the methods of discipline (sila), equanimity (samadhi), and wisdom (prajna). I have not yet interviewed your teacher. He speaks of discipline, equanimity, and wisdom but in what way does he practice it. Tell me so that I may know."

Ch'eng replied, "The Great Master Hsiu says that to refrain from doing any kind of evil is called discipline; that the performance of all kinds of virtues is called wisdom; and that to quiet one's own mind is called equanimity. This is the way he speaks. I have not yet asked, Sir, what method you use to teach people."

The Master replied, "If I should say that I had a method for people I should be deceiving you. It is only that one must unravel entanglements according to the circumstances, and this goes by the name of equanimity in its collective sense. Thus, your teacher may speak of discipline, equanimity, and wisdom, but in reality, it is not possible to conceive them. As I see it, discipline, equanimity, and wisdom are quite different."

Chih Ch'eng said, "There can only be one kind of discipline, equanimity, and wisdom. So, how can there be any difference?"

The Master said, "Your teacher's discipline, equanimity and wisdom are for persons of the Mahayana, but my discipline, equanimity and wisdom are for people of the Supreme Vehicle. The understanding of realization (in these two) is not the same and there are those who are slow in seeing it. Listen to my way of putting it and see whether it is the same as yours or not.

"The Dharma of which I speak is not apart from self-nature. A Dharma apart from this would be called merely formal talk and the self-nature would be always under delusion. You must understand that all the ten thousand dharmas arise and function from self-nature. This is the true doctrine of discipline, equanimity and wisdom.

"Listen to what my poem says:

A mind-ground which criticizes nothing is the
    discipline of self-nature.

126

A mind-ground which attaches itself to nothing
   is the wisdom of self-nature.
A mind-ground without confusion is the equanimity of self-nature.
Neither to augment nor to reduce[3] is the diamond
   of your self-nature.[4]
Whether the physical body is coming or going
   the self-nature remains in equanimity."

Hearing this poem, Ch'eng apologized (to the Patriarch), thanked (him), and presented this poem:

This illusory body of the five skandhas,
Through and through, what an illusion
   it is!
For in the ultimate of true suchness,
Even method[5] becomes a disturbance!

With this, the Master agreed and said to Ch'eng
again, "Your Master's (view) of discipline, equanimity
and wisdom appeals to people whose knowledge has but
slight roots. But my (view of) discipline, equanimity and
wisdom appeals to people of knowledge with great roots.

"If you would realize self-nature, neither set up an
idea of bodhi and nirvana nor set up an idea of the detachment of views.[6] When there is not a single doctrine
to be grasped, then you can firmly set up the ten thousand
doctrines. If you understand this point, this is really to
be called bodhi, nirvana, and the detachment of views.

"A person who has realized his nature sets up ideas
or does not, as he pleases. The ideas come and go freely,
without hesitation or hindrance. They are formulated and
used according to the need that arises. Such words are
employed as are most appropriate for a reply. This is the

127

all-seeing Nirmanakaya which is not different from self-nature. Thence, one attains the divine power of natural mindedness[7] and of vikridita samadhi,[8] and this is called the realization of one's nature."

Chih Ch'eng again respectfully asked the Master saying, "What is the meaning of no-postulation (不立義)?"

The Master replied, "It is when the self-nature is free from criticisms, unattached, and unconfused with the brilliance of bodhi in every thought. (It is when the self-nature) is always free from doctrinal conceptions---and independent and natural. When one has completely realized the depth and the breadth (of Buddhism) in all its perspectives, what is the use of postulating anything?

"When one's self-nature is realized, the realization is instantaneous, the discipline immediate, then there is also neither gradual nor progressive. For this reason, do not postulate any fixed doctrines. When all doctrines and methods have been surpassed, how can there be progressive steps?"

Chih Ch'eng then paid his respects and expressed the desire to be (the Patriarch's) attendant day and night without cessation.

*　　*　　*

There was a monk of Kiangsi called Chih Ch'e,[9] formerly named Chang Hsing Ch'ang (張行昌), a young man inclined to boldness. After the Northern and Southern schools had separated, although the two masters themselves had forgotten the distinctions of Thou and I, there was

128

still rivalry and antipathy among their disciples.

At one time, followers of the Northern school proclaimed their Master Shen Hsiu, to be the Sixth Patriarch. Being envious of the (true) Patriarch, since the fact that he had received the transmission of the robe had become public knowledge, they instructed Hsing Ch'ang to go and stab him. The Master, aware of his intentions before hand, placed ten taels of gold on a chair.

One evening, Hsing Ch'ang came into the Patriarch's room intending injury. Whereupon the Master stretched out his neck to receive it. Hsing Ch'ang lunged at him three times with the knife but not once did he manage to cut him.

The Master said:

> A virtuous sword does not miss.
> A missing sword is not virtuous.
> I owe you only money,
> I do not owe you life.

Hsing Ch'ang fainted in a fright and it was a long time before he regained consciousness. Whereupon, he begged for mercy, repented of his error and expressed his desire to join the order. However, the Master gave him the gold saying, "You had better go away. I am afraid that my disciples might take revenge upon you. Some other day you can change your appearance and come again. I shall then be glad to receive you."

Hsing Ch'ang received this command and then fled by night---afterwards joining the monkhood.

One day he remembered the Master's words and came

from a distance to pay his respects.

The Master said, "I have been thinking of you for a long time. Why have you come so late?"

Hsing Ch'ang replied, "At the time after I received your pardon for my crime, I became a monk and have followed an austere discipline. Yet it is difficult to repay your kindness save by spreading the Dharma among the people. I have constantly studied the Nirvana Sutra, but I do not yet understand the doctrine of permanence and impermanence. Will you, Sir, out of your compassion and forbearance explain it a little?"

The Master said, "Impermanence is the Buddha-nature. Permanence is the mind of discrimination of all virtues and vices, and of all the doctrines."

He replied, "What you have just said, Sir, is a tremendous contradiction of the Sutra."

The Master replied, "I transmit the seal of the Buddha-mind, so how would I dare to contradict the Buddhist sutras?"

Hsing Ch'ang said again, "The Sutra states that the Buddha-nature is permanent but you definitely said that it is impermanent. (The Sutra also says) that good and evil and all the doctrines leading to the awakened mind are entirely impermanent, but you definitely said that they are permanent. These are direct contradictions which set me back again into more doubt and confusion."

The Master answered, "I once heard the nun, Wu Chin Ts'ang, reciting the Nirvana Sutra, and as I discussed it with her (I found) that not a word, not an idea (of mine) was in disagreement with the Sutra. This applies in your case too, for ultimately it must be without dualism."

Ch'ang said, "My capacity for understanding is shallow and dull, but I wish that in spite of this difficulty, you would explain it to me."

The Master said, "Don't you understand? If the Buddha-nature is permanent, of what use would it be to speak further of virtues and vices and of all the various doctrines? For then even after endless kalpas there would not be a single person in whom the bodhi mind would arise。 Therefore, when I speak of impermanence, it is exactly what the Buddha meant when he spoke the doctrine of true permanence.

"Moreover, if absolutely all things are impermanent, then every single one of them would have a (separate) self-nature to undergo birth and death, and then the truly permanent nature would not be universally extended. Therefore, when I speak of permanence, it is exactly what the Buddha meant when he spoke the doctrine of true impermanence.

"The Buddha did this because ordinary people and those not of the Dharma are biased towards a wrong view of permanence. All those who follow the Second Vehicle confused (true) permanence with impermanence and so made the eight upside-down (views).[10] Therefore, the ultimate esoteric meaning of the Parinirvana Sutra is to break up these one-sided views and to expound true permanence, (真常 nitya), true happiness (真樂 sukha), true self-hood (真我 atman), and true purity (真淨 uisuddhi).

"But you by following the mere words have missed the meaning completely and so have taken deliverance to be impermanent and the certainty of death to be permanent, thereby misunderstanding the Buddha's ultimate, marvelous and final analysis. Though you read the Sutra a thousand times, what good will it do you?"

Hsing Ch'ang suddenly entered into the state of great realization and uttered the following poem:

> Because (the uninitiated sought) to control the
>   impermanent mind,
> Whereas the Buddha spoke about the permanent
>   nature.
>
> One who does not understand that this is expedi-
>   ency
> Is like a shallow person picking up pebbles
>   (mistaking them for jewels).
>
> Though I am not now expending effort,
> Yet the Buddha-nature is manifest.
>
> If it were not for the Patriarch's teach-
>   ing,
> I would not have gotten anywhere.

The Master said, "Now, indeed, you understand it thoroughly! I must now call you Chih Ch'e.[9]

Tendering his respectful thanks, Ch'e withdrew.

* * *

The Master observed that (some followers) of various sects were troubling him with questions which arose from their perverse minds and that there were many such who gathered at his sessions. Yet he spoke to them with compassion saying, "Students of the Dharma, all good and evil thoughts should be done away with completely. (There is something) to which no name can be given and we call it self-nature. It is non-dual in nature so we call it the real nature. Upon this real nature all these teachings are firmly established. At the mention of them, you should realize by yourselves."

All who heard these remarks paid homage to him and humbly requested him to be their Master.

FOOTNOTES

1   Ching Nan 荆南
荆 , one of the ancient divisions of China that is now represented
by the provinces of Hunan, 湖南 , Hupeh, 湖北 , and part of
Kweichow, 贵州 . The Yu Ch'uan 玉泉 Monastery was located
at the southern part of this division.

2   Chih Ch'eng 志诚
A native of Chi Chou, 吉州 , a resident of Yu Ch'uan Monastery
and attendant to Shen Hsiu, 神秀 .

3   Neither to augment 不增 , nor to reduce 不减 .
不 , not; 增 , to augment, to add on, to exaggerate, to enlarge.
减 , to reduce, to lessen, to diminish. In its technical sense in
Buddhism, it is used to experience each incident actually as it is, to
see things or persons just as they are without their being augmented
or reduced by any of one's own attachments, dislikes, or precon-
ceived ideas. To do this properly is the beginning of the understanding of suchness 如 .

4   The diamond of your self-nature 自金刚
Diamond, 金刚 , vajra, represents the indestructiveness, the enduring and unchanging quality of one's self-nature.

5   Even method becomes a disturbance 法还不净
法 , methods, dharmas, Dharma, doctrines. In genuine suchness
there is not a single method, thing, or doctrine to be grasped, 无
一法可得 . 法 are methods or ways of practice which, on reaching the goal, are discarded. In the Diamond Sutra Chapter VI, 金刚
经第六 : The Buddha says, " 法尚应舍 . Even the methods (the
doctrines) should be discarded. Because they are like the rafts or
ships to reach the opposite shore, and when you are there, why keep
these methods? Therefore, at this stage, 'even method becomes a
disturbance.'"

6   Detachment of views 解脱知见
The liberation of the mind from all fixed conceptualisms. In this instance, the sutra warns against having even a conception of freeing
the mind from conception.

7   Natural mindedness, 自在 , Isvara.
自 self naturally; 在 , at, on; the words together, 自在 , are the

134

mind as free from hindrances as from delusions. The mind is in its natural state and thus capable of its full power in all aspects.

8 Vikridita samadhi 遊戲三昧
遊戲 , vikridita, play, recreation. 三昧 , samadhi, the ultimate of tranquillity in which enlightenment is attainable.
Thus 遊戲三昧 , is a tranquillity that is so natural that it is like recreation or play---i.e. without restraints.

9 Chih Ch'e 志徹
A native of Kiangsi. His name Ch'e, 徹 , means to understand thoroughly, which accounts for the Master's last remark to him, "I must now call you Chih Ch'e, 志徹 , (determined to understand thoroughly)".

10 Eight upside-down (views) 八倒
The four marks of ordinary life, impermanence, 無常 , anitya; suffering, 苦 , duhkha; selflessness, 無我 , anatman; and impurity, 無淨 , avimala are mistaken by ordinary people and those not of the way to be the four qualities of permanence, pleasure, personality and purity respectively. Those of the Second Vehicle deny the latter now and in nirvana, whereas, the mahayanist asserts permanence in pleasure, personality, and purity are in nirvana.

CHAPTER IX

CHERISHING THE DHARMA

護法品

On January 15, 705 A.D. the Queen Mother Tse T'ien and the Emperor Chung Tsung[1] issued a proclamation saying, "We request An[2] and Hsiu the two masters to receive board and lodging in the palace. When we have leisure from our imperial duties, we would like to study the Ekayana (一乘)."

However, the two masters deferred saying, "Down in the South there is the Pristine Dharma Master Neng who secretly received the robe and Dharma from the Great Master Jen, who transmitted to him the seal of the Buddhamind. You might invite him."

Whereupon they commanded an attendant of the inner palace, Hsieh Chien (薛簡), to be the courier of an edict cordially inviting the Master, desiring him to be compassionately mindful and to come swiftly to the capitol.

The Master submitted his refusal on the grounds that he was ill and wished to spend the rest of his days in his forest at the foot of the hill.

Hsieh Chien said, "Those versed in the Dharma at the capitol say that if one wants to attain an understanding of the Dharma, one must necessarily sit in a state of meditation and practice equanimity. There is no other way of liberation than by means of equanimity. I have not yet questioned you, O Master, what is the doctrine that you

137

teach?"

The Master replied, "(Understanding) of the Dharma is through the awakening of the mind. How can it be through sitting? The Sutra states, 'If anyone says that the Tathagata (the Buddha) should be sitting or should be lying, this is to tread the wrong path.'[3] Why is it that there is nothing that comes and nothing that goes? Because non-arising and non-ceasing is the clear and quiet meditation of the Tathagata (the Buddha).

"(To see) all the things as void and tranquil is the clear and quiet sitting of the Tathagata. Ultimately, there is no fixed criterion. So how can we dare identify it with sitting?"

"When I return to the capitol," said Chien, "their Majesties will certainly question me, so I wish that you, Master, in your kind compassion would point out and instruct me in the essentials of the mind. When I point it out to their Majesties, and those who study the Dharma at the capitol, it will be as if one lamp should light a hundred thousand lamps; then the ignorant ones will all be enlightened, and the enlightened ones' understanding will be limitless."

The Master replied, "In the Dharma there is nothing bright or dark; brightness and darkness have meaning only in its reciprocity. (Although one may speak of) immeasurable brilliance, yet in a literal sense it does have a limit, because the terms, i.e. bright and dark, are mutually opposed. Thus the Vimalakirti Sutra says, 'There is nothing to which the Dharma can be compared, because there are no opposites.'"[4]

"Light," said Chien, "exemplifies wisdom, and darkness exemplifies worries. If one who practices the Dharma does not dissipate worries with the radiance of wisdom, what shall he rely on to be freed from beginningless birth and death?"

The Master replied, "Worries (klesa) is precisely the highest wisdom (bodhi); they are not two and they do not differ. If you dissipate worries with the radiance of wisdom,[5] this is the viewpoint of the Second Vehicle and is in the category of the goats and the deer. (i.e. in the category of the less profound practitioners of the Dharma.) To those of superior wisdom and profound roots, it is not at all like this."

"What, then," asked Chien, "is the view of the Mahayana?"

"The ordinary person," replied the Master, "sees enlightenment and ignorance as two, but the wise one understands thoroughly that his nature is non-dual. This non-dual nature is precisely the genuine nature of reality. This genuine nature-of-reality is not reduced by being in the ignorant nor is it enlarged in the case of sages. While living in the midst of klesa, it is not confused by it. While dwelling in the midst of dhyana and samadhi, it does not become static because of them. It is neither interrupted nor is it permanent. It neither comes nor goes; it is not in the middle nor is it within or without; it does not start (不生); it does not stop (不滅);[6] its essential nature is true suchness (如如) in which it remains forever without wavering. This is what I call the Dharma."

"You say, O Master," asked Chien, "that it neither starts nor stops. Now, how does this differ from (the teaching of) the schismatics?"

"Schismatics," replied the Master, "do indeed speak of not starting and not stopping (of thoughts), but they utilize stopping as putting an end to (the thoughts) which they have started, and they start thoughts so that they can display their ability in stopping them. Therefore, this stopping is not (true) stopping for there is still a starting even though they speak of it as not starting.

"Whereas, I speak in the elemental sense of naturally not starting and at the same time naturally not stopping,[7] and so this is not at all like the teaching of the schismatics. If you wish to know the mind's quintessence, you have only to put a complete stop to concepts of good and evil[8] and then you will have a natural attainment of entrance into the clear and calm body of the mind which is profound yet ever serene. Its marvelous implications are as many as the sands of the Ganges."

Through the favor of these instructions, Chien attained a clear and great awakening. Respectfully taking his leave he returned to the palace and reported to the throne what the Master had said.

On the third of September in that year, an imperial edict was issued, commending and praising the Master, and saying, "Because of age and infirmity, the Master declined (to come to the capitol). Yet, he practices and teaches the Dharma for the benefit of us all. He is indeed a source of the nation's virtues. The Master is like Vimalakirti who had an illness at Vaisali,[9] but he took advantage of the opportunity so that he might expound the Mahayana more widely and transmit the Buddha-mind to all through his discussion of non-duality.

"Hsieh Chien has transmitted the Master's instructions concerning the Tathagata knowledge. We must have accumulated virtues and great merits as a result of planting the virtuous roots in our past karma to have been able to encounter the Master in this life and to have come to such a quick understanding of the Superior Vehicle. We are deeply grateful for the Master's favor and will keep it uppermost (in our mind) without ceasing. We also present him with a Mo Na Robe[10] and a crystal water bowl. We have further issued an edict to the Governor of Shao Province to renovate the monastery buildings as well as the Master's old residence which is to be called the Kuo En Monastery."[11]

FOOTNOTES

1   Queen Mother Tse T'ien (則天) and the Emperor Chung Tsung (中宗)

The Queen Mother Tse T'ien was the actual ruler during the reign of Emperor Chung Tsung. She was in power for twenty-one years.

2   An refers to Hui An 慧安

His full title was 嵩嶽慧安國師 , meaning the Great Hui An, the National Teacher. He was a native of Ching Chou Province, 荆州枝江人 , and had studied under the Fifth Patriarch at Huang Mei (黃梅).

3   From the Diamond Sutra, Chapter XXIX,

金剛經分第二十九

若有人言如來若坐若卧是人行邪道

4   Vimalakirti Sutra says, 'There is nothing to which the Dharma can be compared, because there are no opposites'. 法無有比無相待故

From Vimalakirti Sutra, Chapter III. 淨明經 弟子品第三

5   If you dissipate worries with the radiance of wisdom

若以智慧照破煩惱者

This is a very interesting statement. For, in comparison to those in the beginning stages in the practice, the Sixth Patriarch states that one should use the great wisdom, 大智慧 , to shatter the five skandhas, the defilements, and the turmoils of the gunas in Chapter II. Now when he speaks to Hsieh Chien 薛簡 , and Chien uses practically the same words the Patriarch had used previously, the Patriarch refutes them and says that they do not use prajna. This is because Chien had already understood the meaning at that level, and these instructions of the Sixth Patriarch goes further in their implications.

6   It does not start, it does not stop. 不生不滅

Since the nature-of-reality is beyond duality, it does not initiate thought, and since nothing was started, there is nothing to stop--- nor is there even a concept of not starting and of not stopping.

7   I speak in the elemental sense of naturally not starting and at the same time naturally not stopping--- 本自無生 , 今亦不滅 .

142

Footnotes

Compare this with the profound Vimalakirti Sutra, Chapter III on
The Disciples. 淨明經 , 弟子品第三 . 本自不然 今則無
滅 ; since originally the self-nature has not initiated any thoughts,
then naturally there is now no need of stopping.

8   If you wish to know the mind's quintessence, you have only to put a
     complete stop to concepts of good and evil--- 汝若欲知心要 ，
     但一切善惡都莫思量 .
     Kindly note that this advice is addressed to Hsieh Chien, 薛簡 ,
     who is one of 'those of superior wisdom and profound roots---'. Un-
     less one considers himself to be of superior wisdom and profound roots,
     please do not take this advice. It will do more harm than good.
     Note also that in the earlier Chapters II, III and others, the Patriarch
     refers many times to 除惡 , 離邪 , 'remove the evils, discard the
     erroneous'. For instance, in the Chapter III discussion on the Western
     Paradise, the Patriarch advises the Prefect Wei and others to 先除
     十惡 --- 後除八邪 'first discard the ten evils then discard the
     eight errors', ---. Further, 使若子心地但無不善   ---' that
     one has in his mind nothing that is not virtuous'.
     Such is the prerequisite practice to the stage of the advice given to
     Hsien Chien. If one does not know at what stage he is in he should,
     as the Patriarch says, 須假大善智識示導 , 'seek out a wise
     counselor to point it out to him'.

9   Vaisali 毗耶離
     Vaisali is the location where Vimalakirti had his illness. The Buddha
     knew also that the real purpose of Vimalakirti was to expound the
     Mahayana doctrines. In his compassion he requested each of his ten
     greatest disciples to visit Vimalakirti. The teaching that each dis-
     ciple received from this master formed the basis for an important
     chapter of the Vimalakirti Sutra.

10   Mo Na Robe 磨納袈裟
     It is a special robe that was made in Korea. This is also a traditional
     gift to the Master who transmits the Dharma.

11   Kuo En Monastery 國恩寺
     Boon-to-the-Nation, 國恩 , Monastery 寺 .

CHAPTER X

THE MASTER'S CHARGE TO HIS DISCIPLES
付嘱品

One day the Master summoned his disciples, Fa Hai, Chih Ch'eng, Fa Ta, Shen Hui, Chih Ch'ang, Chih T'ung, Chih Ch'e, Chih Tao, Fa Chen, Fa Ju, and others saying, "All of you surpass the other disciples. After I have passed on, each of you will be the master of a district. I am now going to teach you how to give instructions in the doctrine so that you do not lose the fundamentals of our school.

"It is first necessary to discuss the three categories of this method,[1] and to make active use of the thirty-six pairs of opposites, so that one may pass among them, detached from the two extremes. Whenever you speak of the Dharma do not depart from your self-nature. If someone should suddenly ask you about the Dharma, take the duality in his words to the extreme so as to bring out completely the method of opposition. (For example), coming and going (are seen to) create one another mutually. In the end, the method of duality and opposition are completely removed so that there is nowhere for him to go.

"The contents of the three categories of this method are the aggregates-realms-entrances.[2] As to the aggregates, there are five: form, perception, cognition, mental tendencies and consciousness. As to the entrances, there are twelve: the six external sense qualities of color, sound, odor, taste, stimulus, and incidents, and the six organs---the eyes, ears, nose, tongue, body[3] and mind. As to the realms, there are eighteen: the six qualities, the six organs, and the six forms of consciousness.

"The self-nature is able to encompass the ten thousand things. Then it is called the encompassing-store-consciousness (alayavijnana). If one starts thinking and considering, it is at once turned into the six forms of consciousness. When the six forms of consciousness arise, they pass out through the six organs of sense and perceive the six sense-qualities, and thus it is that the eighteen realms all derive their functions from self-nature. But if the self-nature is biased, it is itself the origin of the errors. If the self-nature is pure, it is the origin of the eighteen virtues. If the function of (self-nature) is evil, the function is that of an ordinary person. But if the function of self-nature is beneficial, the function is that of a Buddha. Whence do these functions arise? They arise from our self-nature.

"As to the reciprocal doctrine of the external, insentient environment, there are five pairs of opposites. They are---heaven versus earth, sun versus moon, light versus darkness, negative versus positive, and water versus fire. As to methods[4] and terminology, there are twelve pairs of opposites. They are---ordinary talk versus the Dharma, affirmation versus negation, shape versus shapelessness, form versus formlessness, defilement versus purity, thing versus voidness, motion versus stillness, clarity versus turbidity, the ordinary versus the wise, monk versus layman, age versus youth, and large versus small. These are the twelve pairs of opposites.

"The self-nature makes use of nineteen pairs of opposites: long versus short, heretic versus orthodox, attachment versus wisdom, ignorance versus knowledge, confusion versus equanimity, mercy versus vengeance, right conduct versus impropriety, honesty versus deviousness, genuine versus false, favoritism versus justice, worries versus enlightenment, permanence versus impermanence, compassion versus cruelty, happiness versus anger, generosity versus avariciousness, progression versus regression, starting versus stopping (of thoughts), the Dharma body versus the physical body, the spiritual body versus the temporal body (i.e. path). Such are the nineteen pairs.

"If," continued the Master, "you understand and use the doctrine of these thirty-six pairs of opposites, then you (will realize) the true principle all through the sutras and the Dharma, and thus in all your comings and goings, you will stay naturally away from the two sides. In the active functioning of your self-nature as in conversations with people, though you are physically in the world of forms, be detached from forms. Though you are spiritually in the void, be detached from the (concept of) void. If you are entirely attached to forms then there is a nurturing of biased views. Yet if you are entirely attached to the void then there is a nurturing of ignorance. The latter, though they say they do not rely on the written scriptures, are making mountains out of nothing and actually are blaspheming the sutras. Since they say that writings are of no use, then people should have no right to speak, because speech itself is necessarily a form of literature. They say, furthermore, that the true Dharma is not founded on words and letters, but this very 'not-founded' are two words and thus already words and letters. When they encounter others talking, they at once sneer at them, saying they are attached to words and letters. You must all recognize that they are self-deluded, which is understandable enough, but in addition they blaspheme the Buddhist sutras. Even without blaspheming the sutras, their guilt is already incalculable!

"If one is attached to external forms or practices a method to seek reality, such as lavish endowments of religious foundations and then discusses the errors and dangers of having given or not given, such a one will not realize his nature for many kalpas.

"Be sure to practice the Dharma as you listen to it, but do not preclude the multiplicity of things from your mind, thereby hindering yourself in regard to the nature of the Dharma. If you merely listen to the discussions of the Dharma but do not practice it, you are causing people to have erroneous thoughts and ideas of criticisms. Be sure to put the Dharma into practice and in your teaching of the Dharma do not dwell on forms. If all of you realize this, then be in accord with the Dharma in your speech; be in accord with it in all your usages; be in accord with it in your mind's functions; be in accord with it in all your activities. Then you will not lose the Pristine Orthodox Dharma.

"If someone in asking you a question, asks about 'having thoughts', answer with 'no-thought'; if someone asks about 'no-thought', reply with 'unattached thoughts'. If one asks about the unenlightened, answer in terms of the sage; if one asks about the sage, answer in terms of the unenlightened. By this method of mutually related pairs arises an understanding of the middle way. For every question that you are asked, respond in terms of its opposite. If you deal with all other questions in accordance with this method you surely will not lose the doctrines.

"Suppose that someone asks, 'What is it that we call darkness?' Answer by saying, 'Light is the cause,[5] darkness is the condition.[6] When light ceases then there is darkness, for it takes light to manifest darkness, and darkness to manifest light. Their coming and going are mutually interdependent; this constitutes the meaning of the middle way.' Answer all other questions in like fashion.

In transmitting the Dharma, all of you should hereafter teach in accordance with this method of reciprocal relationship. Do not lose the fundamentals of the doctrines."

In July 692 A.D., the Master ordered his disciples to go to the Kuo En Monastery in Hsin Chou Province to build a pagoda. He urged them that the work be done quickly. It was completed at the end of the summer in the following year. On the first of July 693 A.D., he gathered all his disciples together and said, "I wish to depart from this world in August. If any of you still harbor doubts you should ask about them at the earliest opportunity, so that I may resolve them for you and enable your delusions to be ended. For when I am gone, there will be no one to teach you."

Upon hearing this Fa Hai and the others all had tears in their eyes. Only Shen Hui remained unmoved by emotions and showed no tears.

The Master said, "Little Master Shen Hui has certainly attained equality towards good and evil. He is unmoved by insults or praises; he does not start up thoughts at sadness or happiness. The rest of you have not attained this. You have been here in these mountains for several years. But what kind of teachings have you actually been practicing?

"Here you are crying in sorrow---but for whom are you grieving? If you grieve because I do not know where I am going (you should remember) that I myself am aware of where I am going. If I did not, I could never have foretold it to you. You are all sad and tearful because you do not know where I am going. If you did know, you would realize fully that tears and sadness are not at all appropriate.

149

"Moreover, fundamentally the Dharma-nature has no starting or stopping, no coming or going. Will all of you please sit down? I am going to compose a poem for you which will be called the poem of Reality and Illusion, Perturbation and Serenity. If you all get the point of this poem and observe it, your grasp of its meaning will be the same as mine. If you will put this into practice, you will not lose the essence of the doctrine."

Making obeisance, all of the monks asked the Master to compose the poem.

The poem said:

All things are without reality;
So do not regard them as real.

If one regards them as real,
This itself is a completely unreal view-
    point.

If you can attain reality by yourself,
Prescinding illusions, will leave the re-
    ality of the mind itself.

But if the mind itself is not free from
    illusions,
There is no reality.
So where will you find reality?

Sentient beings react emotionally,
But the insentient cannot react.

If you practice the discipline of non-
    reaction,
This is just the same as the non-reaction

of the insentient.

If you seek for the true non-reaction,
It is the non-reaction of reaction.

Non-reaction alone is just no reaction,
Insentient, without potentiality of Buddhahood.

The capacity to discern situations skillfully
Is the ultimate meaning of non-reaction.

But only act in accordance with this
view,
And you will have at once the functioning of true suchness.

I am announcing to every student of the
Dharma!
That exerting yourselves requires think-
ing.

Do not stand at the gate of the Mahayana,
Only to cling to the simple knowledge
of life and death.

If a person is responsive at the first words,
You can discuss with him the meaning
of Buddhism.

But if he is decidedly unresponsive,
Greet him with your palms respectfully
together wishing him happiness.

It is a fundamental principle of our school

151

not to argue;
To argue is to lose the meaning of the
way.

In bigoted, perverse argumentative teachings,
The self-nature plunges into the cycle of life
and death.

As soon as the assembled disciples had heard this poem,
they all made obeisance. With deep respect for the Master's
intentions and message, all of them disciplined themselves
in accordance with the Dharma. No one dared to argue
again.

Knowing, furthermore, that the Great Master had not
much longer to remain in this world, Fa Hai came forward
to a high seat and paying his respects again, asked him,
saying, "Reverend Sir, after you have entered into nirvana,
to whom should the robe and Dharma be entrusted?"

The Master replied, "Record and disseminate the
teachings which I have given at the Ta Fan Monastery until this present time. Entitle it The Altar Sutra on the
Pristine Orthodox Dharma.[7] Guard and cherish it all of
you, transmitting and teaching it from one to another for-
the deliverance of all sentient beings. Only what is in
accord with what I have spoken is to be called the Orthodox Dharma.

"At this time (it is fitting) that I should teach the
Dharma for all your sakes and not for the transmitting of
the robe. It is entirely due to the fact that the roots of
your belief are genuine and mature, and that you are decisively and definitely free from doubts, that you are fit
for the great task (of teaching the Dharma). As evident
by the meaning of the transmission poem of the First Patri-

arch, Bodhidharma, it is not appropriate that the robe be transmitted anymore. The poem said:

My purpose in coming to this land
Is to transmit the Dharma for the
help of the deluded.
When the flower has blossomed five
times,
The fruit will ripen of itself---
naturally."

The Master continued, "If all of you wish your seeds of knowledge to ripen, you should know the tranquil-equanimity of unified perspective (一相三昧) and the tranquil-equanimity of unified practice (一行三昧). If you can be in all places without attachment to forms, if you can be in the midst of forms and not give rise to disliking and liking, nor to grasping or releasing, nor to consider (your own) benefits or losses, nor matters of successes or failures; (if you can be) calm, casual, tranquil, humble, adaptable, serene, and quiet, this is called the tranquil-equanimity of unified perspective.

"Whether walking, standing, sitting or lying down, if you can in all places be simple and straightforward in mind, without reminding yourself to be in the realm of the Dharma, then you have truly attained the pure land of your mind. This is called the tranquil-equanimity of unified practice. If a person is perfect in these two tranquil-equanimities, he is like the soil in which the seeds, covered and buried, grow up and are nourished to the ripening of their fruit. Unified perspective and unified practice are just like that.

"My present teaching of the Dharma is like the seasonable rain which nourishes the great earth everywhere.

153

Your Buddha-nature resembles those seeds which, as they receive this beneficent moisture, will all begin to grow. Those who accept my teaching will definitely attain bodhi. If they follow my practice they will certainly manifest its wondrous fruit. Listen to what my poem says:

> The mind-ground embraces a multitude
>   of seeds;
> With the universal rain they will all
>   sprout.
> Quickly realize the significance of the
>   flower,[8]
> Then the fruit of bodhi will ripen of
>   itself."

When the Master had spoken this poem he said, "The Dharma is without duality: so also is the mind. Its practice is clear and quiet and free from the multiplicity of forms. You must be most careful not to repress yourself to quietness nor to force a completely emptied mind. For the mind is basically quiet; there is nothing to be retained or to be renounced. Let everyone of you exert yourself and go forward in accordance with the appropriateness of the conditions." Thereupon, the assembled disciples paid their respects and withdrew.

On July 8th, the Great Master suddenly said to his disciples, "I want to go back to Hsin Chou. Will you quickly prepare the boat and oars?" The whole group earnestly entreated him to stay.

But the Master replied:

> All the Buddhas manifest themselves
> Only for the revelation of nirvana.
> That which comes must go;

The law is ever thus.
Mine is also but a physical body.
It must return to its place.

"Master," they said, "when you have gone from here, will you eventually return?"

The Master replied:

When the leaves fall
They return to the place of their roots.
When I return
I will have no mouth (to speak 来時無口 .)

They asked again saying, "To whom will the Resolving-Vision of the Orthodox Dharma (正法眼藏 i.e. the perfect perspective of viewing virtue without being over-joyed and of evil without being angry be transmitted).

The Master replied:

Those who have the Dharma will attain it.
Those who have the unattached mind will
understand it.

"We do not yet know," they said, "through how many generations the teachings have been transmitted from the manifestation of the first Buddha until now. We wish you would be so kind as to explain this."

The Master said, "Since ancient times Buddhas have entered into the world without number and cannot be counted. Today, we must take the Seven Buddhas to be the beginning. In the past alamkaraka kalpa[9] there were:

I   Vipasyin Buddha
昆婆尸佛

II   Sikhin Buddha
尸棄佛

III Visvabhu Buddha
毗舍浮佛

Now, in the present, the good kalpa (賢叔 Bhadra):

IV   Krakucchanda Buddha
拘留孫佛

V   Kanakamuni Buddha
拘那含牟尼佛

VI   Kasyapa Buddha
迦葉佛

VII Sakyamuni Buddha is the Seventh Buddha
釋迦文佛

Sakyamuni Buddha transmitted to

The First (Patriarch, India): Mahakasyapa Arya
摩訶迦葉尊者

The Second: (Patriarch) Ananda Arya
阿難尊者

The Third: Sanavasa Arya
商那和修尊者

The Fourth: Upagupta Arya
優波毱多尊者

The Fifth: Dhrtaka Arya
提多迦尊者

The Sixth: Mikkaka Arya
彌遮迦尊者

The Seventh: Vasumitra Arya
婆須密多尊者

The Eighth: Buddhanandi Arya
佛馱難提尊者

The Ninth: Buddhamitra Arya
伏馱密多尊者

The Tenth: Parsva Arya
脅尊者

The Eleventh: Punyayasas Arya
富那夜奢尊者

The Twelfth: Asvaghosa Mahasattva
馬鳴大士

The Thirteenth: Kapimala Arya
迦毗摩羅尊者

The Fourteenth: Nagarjuna Mahasattva
龍樹大士

The Fifteenth: Kanadeva Arya
迦那提婆尊者

The Sixteenth: Rahulata Arya
羅睺羅多尊者

The Seventeenth: Sanghanandi Arya
僧伽難提尊者

The Eighteenth: Gayasata Arya
伽耶舍多尊者

The Nineteenth: Kumarata Arya
鳩摩羅多尊者

The Twentieth: Jayata Arya
闍耶多尊者

The Twenty-first: Vasubandhu Arya
婆修盤頭尊者

The Twenty-second: Manorhita Arya
摩拏羅尊者

The Twenty-third: Haklena Arya
鶴勒那尊者

The Twenty-fourth: Simha Arya
師子尊者

The Twenty-fifth: Basiasita Arya
婆舍斯多尊者

The Twenty-sixth: Punyamitra Arya
不如密多尊者

The Twenty-seventh: Prajnatara Arya
般若多羅尊者

The Twenty-eighth: Bodhidharma Arya
菩提達摩尊者

In this land (i.e. China) he is the First Patriarch.

The Twenty-ninth: Hui K'o the Great Master
    (or the Second Patriarch)
    慧可大師

The Thirtieth: Seng Ts'an the Great Master
    (or the Third Patriarch)
    僧璨大師

The Thirty-first: Tao Hsin the Great Master
    (or the Fourth Patriarch)
    道信大師

The Thirty-second: Hung Jen the Great Master
    (or the Fifth Patriarch)
    弘忍大師

and Hui Neng is the Thirty-third Patriarch 惠能
大師 (or the Sixth Patriarch), who is the last one.

"Each of the patriarchs listed above has his designated successor (to the Dharma). Hereafter, you will all continue its flow as a group, and be sure not to let it be misinterpreted."

They asked again, "We won't have any difficulty from now on, will we?"

"Five or six years after my death," the Master replied, "there will be a person who will want to get hold of my head. Hear my prophecy which says:

His appearance will be most pious
But he will be acting out of need for
    sustenance.

159

When this problem of 'Man'[10] arises,
Yang and Liu are the officials!"

On August 3, 713A.D., the Great Master was at the Kuo En Monastery. After fasting he addressed the whole assembly of his disciples.

"Will all of you please sit down according to rank. I am about to take leave of you."

Respectfully Fa Hai addressed him, "Venerable Sir, what method of instruction will you leave behind for future generations so that the unawakened people may attain the realization of their Buddha-nature?"

The Master replied, "Listen carefully, all of you. In regard to these unawakened people of future times: if they truly know the ordinary nature, this is precisely to know Buddha-nature. If they have no true knowledge of the ordinary nature, it will be hard to meet the Buddha even when sought for ten thousand kalpas. I shall now instruct you how to know your ordinary mind in such a way as to realize the Buddha-nature in your own mind.

"If you want to seek the realization of the Buddha you must gain a true knowledge of ordinary nature. It is because the ordinary obscures the Buddha-nature and not that the Buddha-nature obscures the ordinary. If you realize your self-nature, the ordinary person is a Buddha. If your self-nature is unawakened, the Buddha is the ordinary person.

"When one's self-nature is in a state of equality then the ordinary nature is the Buddha-nature. When one's self-nature is treacherously biased, then the Buddha-nature is the ordinary. If all your minds are treacherously awry,

160

then the Buddha-nature is (hidden) within the ordinary. In a single, even, and straightforward thought, the ordinary person becomes a Buddha.

"Our own mind is of itself a Buddha. This natural Buddha is the real Buddha. If there is no Buddha in one's mind, where shall the real Buddha be sought? All of you! Your own mind is the Buddha! Have no further doubt of it! Externally there is not a single thing able to stand by itself. Everything is fundamentally the mind which starts up the ten thousand kinds of things. Thus the Sutra[11] says, 'When the mind starts up, all the various things arise. When the mind ceases, all the various things cease.'

"In taking leave of you I shall now bequeath a poem which is called 'Self-nature is the Real Buddha.' People of future generations, who thoroughly understand the meaning of this poem, will of themselves see into their original mind and will of themselves attain Buddha-hood. The poem says:

> The true suchness of self-nature is the real Buddha.
> Biased views and the three poisons are the Mararaja.[12]
>
> When there is bias and delusion, Mara rules the house,
> But when there are perfect views, the Buddha presides.
>
> When biased views and the three poisons arise in our nature,
> It is then that the Mararaja comes to live in the house (mind).

The perfect views naturally remove the three
    poisons from the mind,
Mara changes completely into Buddha, truly
    and without pretense.

As for the Dharmakaya, Sambhogakaya and
    Nirmanakaya,
These three bodies are fundamentally one.

If you can realize them within your own
    nature,
It is to perfect one's change to the Buddha's
    awakening.

Fundamentally the Nirmanakaya gives birth
    to the pure nature:
The pure nature is eternally within the Nir-
    manakaya.

The Nirmanakaya of such a nature naturally
    follows only the virtuous Dharma:
Therefrom arises the perfect Sambhogakaya
    truly and without limit.

The turbulent nature is the original source
    of the pure nature,
And when lusts are removed there at once
    is the pure nature's body.

When this nature within each one of you is
    of itself detached from the five de-
    sires, [13]
The realization of this nature becomes in-
    stantaneously the precise Reality.

If in this life you encounter the teaching of

the Sudden School,
You can suddenly realize your self-nature
and see the world-honored Buddha.

However, when you want a specific discipline to become a Buddha,
Then you will not know the point of depar-
ture for seeking Reality.

If within your own mind you can behold the
Reality of your self-nature,
Such a Reality is the origin of perfect Bud-
dhahood.

However, not to realize self-nature thusly,
but to try and seek the Buddha externally,
Means one is from the very beginning a
totally, ignorant person.

I have now already bequeathed to you the
method of the Sudden School,
And the deliverance of all people depends
on each practicing it for oneself.

Let me tell you future students of the Dharma,
If you do not practice these views you will
be more and more remote (from the
truth)."

Having uttered this poem, the Master said, "Pay close
attention all of you. After I have passed away, do not
follow the worldly custom of grief and weeping. Neither
receive expressions of condolences, nor wear mourning.
Such are not my disciples nor are these activities consis-
tent with the true Dharma.

"Do realize your own original mind and see into your original nature which should never be self-witnessing its own imperturbability and equanimity. It neither starts up (thoughts) nor stops (them). Neither is it deluded by worldly thoughts as they come nor is it attached to them as they go. Neither is it in accord with, nor is it (then or thereafter) critical of (others' errors). It is neither attached to nor does it drive away (fallacious concepts).

"For fear that your mind may still be under delusion, and thus unable to understand my deeper meaning, I instruct you once more in order that you may see into your own nature. After I have passed away, maintain this in practice just as if I were still with you. Because if you go against the teaching, it would be of no benefit to you, even if I were still in this world." Once again he spoke a poem saying:

Calm and serene, not by constantly practicing
the virtues (but only as the occasion
arises.)
Harassed and beseiged---yet not to do evil.
Tranquility and peacefulness --- through the
prescinding of biased views.
Through any cyclic waves of life---yet the
mind has no attachments.

Having uttered this poem, the Master in full serenity, sat until the third watch. Suddenly he said to his disciples, "Now I shall leave". And thence it was that he left this mortal life. Whereupon, an ineffable fragrance filled the house and a glowing rainbow illuminated the ground. The trees of the forest reflected the light while birds and beasts cried out in mourning.

That November, government officials, disciples and

laymen of the three provinces of Kwang, Shao, and Hsin debated as to the disposal of his body, being undecided as to where to lay it to rest. Wherefore, they lit incense and prayed saying, "As the incense wafts towards the area, there shall the Master abide."

The incense floated directly to Ts'ao Ch'i. On November the thirteenth, they moved the shrine, the robe, and the bowl back to Ts'ao Ch'i.

On July 25th of the following year, they were taken out of the shrine, and the disciple Fang P'ien devotedly embalmed the body with fragrant clay. Recalling the prophecy of an attempt to steal the head, the disciples protected the Master's neck first with iron plates and then firmly wrapped lacquer cloth around the body, before placing it back in the stupa. Suddenly a white light radiated forth from within the stupa and went straight up into the skies remaining for three days before it dispersed. (The officials) of Shao Chou reported it to the throne. They received and executed an imperial edict to set up tablets of stone bearing a record of the Master's following of the Dharma.

The Master attained an age of seventy-six years. The robe was transmitted to him at the age of twenty-four. He received the tonsure at the age of thirty-nine and taught the Dharma for the benefit of all mankind for thirty-seven years. (As a result of which) forty-three persons grasped the fundamental principles and inherited the Dharma, while innumerable others awakened to the teachings and rose above the ordinary.

The robe of faith, the Mo Na Robe, which had been handed down from Bodhidharma, the precious bowl presented by the Emperor Tsung, the effigy of the Master fashioned by Fang P'ien, together with other ritual objects were entrusted to the supervising attendant of the stupa and are perpetually guarded at Pao Lin Monastery.

May this Altar Sutra of the Pristine Orthodox Dharma flow forth to reveal the principles of this school! Let the three gems flourish for the benefit of all mankind!

*   *   *

FOOTNOTES

1   Three categories of the method 三科法門
    法門 , Dharmaparyaya, the doctrine, method, dharma. In this
    case---method. 三科 , the three categories, which are divided
    into: (1) 五蘊 , the five skandhas or aggregates. (2) 十二入 ,
    twelve-sense-gates. (3) 十八界 , eighteen realms.

2   Aggregates-realms-entrances. See Footnote X-1.

3   Body 身 , this is the body as a whole when considered as an organ
    of sensation.

4   Methods, 法相 , dharmalaksana.

5   Light is the cause, 明是因 , hetu, 因 .
    Light, or understanding, when not present is the cause of darkness or
    ignorance. When there is understanding or light there is correspond-
    ing lessening of ignorance or darkness. Thus, light or rather the ab-
    sence of light is the proximate cause (hetu) of the resulting incident
    (pratyaya) of darkness.

6   Condition (Incident), pratyaya. See Footnote X-5.

7   法寶壇禪經

8   The significance of the flower.
    This refers to the time the Buddha, (while in front of all his most ad-
    vanced disciples) smilingly held a flower in his hand without saying
    a word to represent the highest practice, the most essential principle
    of the Pristine Dharma.

9   Alamkaraka kalpa 莊嚴劫
    莊嚴 , alamkaraka, adorn, glory, honor, ornate; e.g. the adorn-
    ments of morality, meditation, wisdom, and the control of good and
    evil forces.
    莊嚴劫 . The glorious kalpa to which more than a thousand Bud-
    dhas, one succeeding another, have brought their most accomplished
    attainment in morality, meditation, and wisdom towards the formu-
    lation of the Dharma.

10 Man 滿
    The name of the person who will come for the Patriarch's head is

167

Chang Ching Man, 張淨滿

11 The Sutra says: When the mind starts up, all the various things arise. When the mind ceases, all the various things cease. 心生 ，種種 法生；心滅，種種法滅 . From Surangama Sutra; Chapter I, 楞嚴經 . This statement was made by the Buddha in response to the question by 阿難 , Ananda.

12 Mara raja 魔王
Mara, killing, destroying; 王 , king; the king of the destroyers, or the king of the malignant ones. Though sometimes otherwise defined, the Patriarch explains mara as biased views and greed, anger and attachments.

13 Five desires 五欲
The five desires, arising from the objects of the five senses: sight 色 ; sound 聲 ; odor 香 ; taste 味 ; stimulus 觸 .

GLOSSARY A

ENGLISH, SANSKRIT AND CHINESE

Alayavijnana आलयविज्ञान 阿賴耶識
'Stored-consciousness'. "The receptacle intellect or consciousness"; "the originating or receptacle intelligence"; "basic consciousness" (Keith). It is the store or totality of consciousness, both absolute and relative. It is the storehouse of experience, of the skandhas, and of all things on which sentient beings depend for existence.

Arising and ceasing, utpadanirodha उत्पादनिरोध 生滅
1. Birth and death, production and annihilation; all life, all phenomena, have birth and death, beginning and end.
2. In this sutra, this term is frequently used in application to the arising and ceasing of thought processes. The principle is---why spend time annihilating unnecessary or erroneous thoughts when all one has to do is just not evoke or produce them.

Awakening 悟
Awakening, great 大悟
悟 awakening, to apprehend, to perceive, to have insight. It implies a power to know immediately. In its use in Buddhism it means the direct insight into one's own mind, the knowledge being of such an immediate nature that it is called an awakening. It is as if one had actually been asleep all the time up till then. The awakening may be temporary but the 'great awakening' connotes a state wherein one does not lapse back into the condition of ignorance anymore.

Biased views 邪見
邪 slanted, distorted, biased, warped.
見 to see, view, conceptions.
So---biased views are those that are not the proper or the correct ones. They are views based on attachments, anxieties, and misconceptions, and thus are slanted away from the truth.

Bodhi, wisdom बोधि 菩提
Bodhi (from the word budh) means knowledge, understanding, and perfect wisdom. It is also the name of the tree under which the Buddha attained enlightenment, the Bodhi Tree.

Bodhisattva बोधिसत्व 菩薩
Refers to a Buddhist whose purpose is not dedicated to his own salvation but that of all mankind. A person who has attained Buddhahood but still lives like an ordinary person so that he may help others to

171

find their way out of suffering. This is considered a distinguishing characteristic of the Mahayana School.

Buddha-nature, Buddhata बुद्दता 佛性

It means the innate nature in everyone of enlightenment or gnosis, or Buddhahood. Though this potentiality is inherent in all, it requires the assiduous cultivation of virtuous roots before its fruit can ripen.

Clear and quiet, parisuddhi परिशुद्दि 清淨

清 amala, pure, clear. 淨 vimala, clean, quiet, pure.

清淨 parisuddhi, visuddhi. This is a state wherein one's mind is clear and quiet, free from any evil or defilement or anxiety. This is also the original state of our self-nature. It is only by the complete removal of any evil and erroneous thoughts can this original state be attained.

Conditioning (Incident), pratyaya प्रत्यय 緣

In Buddhism this carries the special meaning of a conditioning or circumstantial cause of an occasion or event. In contrast, 因 , hetu, is the proximate, direct cause. An example of 因緣 , hetu-pratyaya, or causality that is frequently used is that of pratyaya as the favorable soil to the hetu, as the seed. Causality is also used to mean an affinity, a causal relation.

Defilements, klesa क्लेश 煩惱 also 塵勞

They are the cares, troubles, afflictions of the passions and of the ignorance which disturbs and beclouds the mind; also in brief, as the three poisons 貪瞋癡 desire, detestation, and delusion. These are the roots from which the many varieties of anxieties arise---so many that they are usually referred to as "84,000" 八萬四千 .

Deliverance, paramita पारमिता 度

To pass, to cross over, to ferry over ('the ocean of birth and death') also to save (other beings) 度眾生 . It refers to the practice by which one is enabled to reach the opposite shore. As the Sixth Patriarch says it means the 'letting go of the starting and stopping of thoughts'.

Deluded, maya माया 迷

Delude, deceive, confuse; delusion, illusion. Used in the sense of being under the delusion that the impermanence of the everyday world is permanent. Thus this world of maya i.e. the world of delu-

172

sions.

Devas, heaven   देव   天
Sky; a day; also deva, meaning a devine being, the celestial world.

Dharmadhatu   धर्मधातु   法界
The dharmadhatu or dharma-realm
1. A term used sometimes for all noumenal or phenomenal things.
2. A term also used for a person's being open to Buddha-wisdom as
開法界 , or opening one's own dharma-realm after one has attained enlightenment.

Dharmakaya   धर्मकाय   法身
The spiritual or true body. The embodiment of the Truth and Law.
The first of the three bodies, the Trikaya 三身 . This is said of the
three bodies of the Buddha but in Chapter VI, Hui Neng shows that
it is in one's self-nature when the delusions are gotten rid of and
there is clear understanding both within and without.

Discipline, sila   शील   戒
See precepts

Ekayana   एकयान   一乘
Eka, 一 , meaning one, unity   एक
yana, 乘 , vehicle   यान
Thus, the one vehicle. The complete, the total vehicle. Sometimes
this is inferred to be the Mahayana, as being the complete and final
stage of Buddhism. However, as the Sixth Patriarch says 'the Buddha
really spoke only 一佛乘 , one-Buddhist-yana'. (See Saddharma
Pundarika Sutra, 法華經). But because of the varying capacities
of people it is divided into further classes as a form of upaya 方便 .
(Also see Chapter VII of the Sutra on the conversation between the
Sixth Patriarch and Fa Ta 法達).

Encumbrances, varana, avarana   आवरण   障
A screen, a barricade, a partition; or a term for the passions or any
delusion which hinders enlightenment. It also includes the connota-
tion of one's past karma with its many wrong patterns of thought that
frequently arise in us to thwart our treading the right path. Usually
this is in the form of concepts which are wrong but which we cannot
realize ourselves. Thus, these become barricades to our further enlightenment.

Glossary A

Field of merit　福田

　　The sphere of blessings, good fortune and merits. It implies a karmic qualification that one does good for the sake of the reward. On the other hand, an advanced Buddhist should be beyond that stage. He should be then a 'sphere of virtue for mankind', 為興眾生作福田 .

Formal phenomena, Dharmalaksana　धर्मलक्षण

　　1. The aspects, characteristics and forms of all things
　　2. that all things have but one nature, differing only in form.
　　3. Also the perspective of the Dharma, i.e. that one has a 'grasp of' the Dharma. If one has such, then one should 捨 , let it go.

Formless, 'No-form', animatta, nirabhasa　निराभास　無相

　　無 no, none;
　　相 form, shape, perspectives, formality, external appearance.
　　Formless, 無相 , infers the unreality, the artificiality of forms and phenomena. Thus, formless would mean the absence of any artificiality of ritual or formality. It would mean that the practice or the word is directly within and from one's heart and mind.

Fortune 福
Discipline oneself for the sake of fortune 修福

　　This word is commonly but erroneously used for merit-virtue 功德 . 修福 , disciplining oneself for the sake of fortune, is the charge that the Sixth Patriarch makes of all deluded persons. One who performs charity of any kind when it carries with it the intent that it will make oneself better either in this world or elsewhere is disciplining oneself for fortune. This implies a reward. Thus 福 or 福德 should never be confused with 功德 merit-virtue which not only has no such implication, but also carries with it the definite requirement of clearing one's heart and mind of all erroneous thinking. For further discussion, see beginning of Chapter III and the poem at the end of Chapter VI. Also see Footnote III-2.

Four classes　चतुर्वर्ग　四眾

　　The four vargas(groups or orders) 四眾 , i.e. 比邱 bhiksu, monks; 比邱尼 bhiksuni, nuns; 優婆塞 upasaka, male devotees; and 優婆夷 , upasika, female devotees. The latter two groups being those who are living with their families, the former two, in monasteries and convents.

174

Four elements 四大
The four elements of which all things are made; i.e. 地 earth; 水 water; 火 fire; and 風 wind (or air). They represent 堅 solid; 濕 liquid; 煖 heat; and 動 motion.

Four relations, four avastha, or the four perspectives 四相 .
In 禪宗 in Ch'an Buddhism, 我相 ; the perspective of self, 不可 自私和自利 ; one must not be selfish or self seeking.
人相 ; perspective of others, 除痛癢無關 , discard the attitude that sufferings of others is of no concern.
衆生相 ; perspective of humanity, 斷除範圍 , 分形絕界 , break and remove all barriers so as not to separate any other human being regardless of color, creed, or country from one's concern.
壽者相 ; perspective of self in future, 明瞭修道無求無得 , one must understand that in the practice of Buddhism, there is neither seeking nor attaining, i.e. there is nothing to be sought as a goal or reward, so there is no such attainment.

Four wisdoms 四智
The four forms of wisdom of a Buddha are:
1. 大圓鏡智 , the great-round-mirror-wisdom.
2. 平等性智 , the even-natured-wisdom.
3. 妙觀察智 , the marvelous-contemplation-wisdom.
4. 成所作智 , the action-perfecting-wisdom.

Gunas, dust, quality गुण 塵
In Sanskrit, the meaning is a quality---a secondary element. In Chinese the literal meaning is dust, small particle. Symbolically, it means the troubles of our everyday living. When the word is used in combination with 勞 it is synonymous with klesa.
It is also used as 六 (six) 塵 , then it means the six sense qualities, or the six gunas which are sight, hearing, smell, taste, touch and thought. More specifically, the reference is to the objects that stir these functions rather than the functions themselves.

Hetupratyaya, conditioning, causative incident हेतुप्रत्यय 因緣
In Buddhism this carries the special meaning of a conditioning or circumstantial cause of an occasion or event. In contrast, 因 hetu, is the proximate, direct cause. An example of 因緣 , hetupratyaya, or causality that frequently is used is that of pratyaya as the favorable soil to the hetu, as the seed. Thus the seed needs the soil for

it to grow. The soil needs the seeds for it to nourish. It is a mutually related situation. From this comes causality or hetupratyaya to
mean a causal relation, an affinity. 因緣 is thus used in 因緣説
法 , to have a causal reason (i.e. a question or request) before
speaking the Dharma.

Intellect 意

Manas is the sixth of the sadayatanas a term which means both the
organ and the sensory functions, i.e. eye, ear, nose, tongue, body
and mind, and its functions. One function of manas is to act as the
correlator of the functions and the responses of the first five senses.
Another function is that of being the intellect---the conscious mental activity. It is intellection based upon one's knowledge, learning,
and experiences of this lifetime.

Jnana ज्ञान 智

Knowledge; wisdom; defined as 於事理決斷也 decision or judg-
ment as to phenomena or affairs and their principles, of things and
their fundamental laws. Also see four wisdoms, and Footnote VII-19.

Kalpa कल्प 刧

Aeon, age---a fabulous period of time. Also, a lifetime.

Karma कर्म 因果

Its Sanskrit meaning is action. From this have come its meaning of
of cause and effect or as in the Chinese cause 因 and results 果 .
It means that our lives are the results of our past thoughts and actions.
Our future is created by our thoughts and actions of the present.

Ksamayati क्षमयति 懺悔

See Footnote VI-2

Mahaprajnaparamita महाप्रज्ञापारमिता 摩訶般若波羅密多

Maha 摩訶 great; prajna 般若 wisdom; paramita 波羅密多 de-
rived from parama, the highest, the acme; thus Mahaprajnaparamita
means the great wisdom method of reaching that opposite shore, i.e.
complete enlightenment.

Mahayana महायान 大乘

See Yana.

Mano-vijnana मनोनिज्ञान 末那識

Manah; manas; intp. by 意 mind, the (active) mind. The 末那識 is defined by the Treatise of the Vijnanas 唯識論 , as the seventh of the 八識 , namely 意 , which means 思量 thinking and measuring, or calculating. It is the active mind, or activity of mind but is also used for the mind itself. See also Footnote VII-19.

Meditation, dhyana ध्यान 坐禅

Dhyana is a method of meditation wherein in the beginning one sits quietly so that his mind becomes calm and peaceful. The purpose is to understand and to gain a greater view of his own mind in order that this equanimity can be carried throughout the day. It is also to attain more enlightenment into one's daily activities to see where one has strayed from the path. For further discussion of this practice, see Fung and Fung, Tso-Ch'an I, American Academy of Asian Studies, San Francisco, 1954.

Merit-virtue 功德

功 , merit, meritorious; 德 , virtue, moral excellence. In Buddhist terminology, this has some special implications. 功德 merit-virtue, implies not only that benevolent actions are done without any expectation of reward but also the inward merits which pertain to the freeing of one's mind from all attachments, delusions, and erroneous views back to its original, pristine status of clarity and quietude.
This is frequently confused as did Emperor Wu with 福 wealth 德 virtue. This is the usual performance of good deeds to which are attached some degree of expectation of reward. Since this reward is usually in good fortune, it is called 福德 to which we shall apply the term 'karmic-virtue'. But the most important fact is that there is not an accompanying discipline of the mind in these activities so they cannot be called 功德 merit-virtue, which is the point of the Patriarch's discussion. To clarify these distinctive points, we are using the full terms of merit-virtue for 功德 rather than just merits, because it is important that these differences be clearly understood.

Mind 心

The word 心 has various meanings, one of which is the anatomical one of the physical heart, of which the character itself is not unlike a schematic diagram. It also refers to the heart as the site of thinking and emotions in its non-physical sense and thus as the mind. In the latter sense, it is construed to be the storehouse of all one's past thought-patterns good or bad. The clearing up of this to its pure original state reveals the self-nature.

Mystery 玄

玄 , abstruse, occult, dark, obscure, deep and profound. A term used both by Taoists and Buddhists.

Nirmanakaya निर्माणकाय 化身佛

One of the three bodies of the Trikaya, 三身 . A Buddha's metamorphic body which has the power to assume any shape to propagate the Truth. In this sutra, the Sixth Patriarch shows that our own self-nature has 'a multitude of transformation of which the deluded person is unaware'. If all these erroneous thoughts are cleared away and prajna arises we, too, can have 'the Nirmanakaya Buddha of self-nature'.

Nirvana निर्वाण 涅槃

Literally, the Sanskrit means 'blown-out, extinguished, dead, deceased'. But its use in Buddhism is not quite the same. Here, it means that it is a state of mind, where there is neither arising 無生 nor ceasing 無滅 . Moreover, there is no concept of non-arising or ceasing 無生滅想 . In this sense, it is very much like 寂滅 , tranquil cessation, but Nirvana is not tranquil cessation. The latter is a practice towards nirvana. In the natural arising and ceasing of thoughts, tranquil cessation may still have some 氣味 , some semblance of a 'whiff of flavor'. But in nirvana, there is utterly no remnant of arising or non-arising of ceasing or non-ceasing. It is the 無如涅槃 (see Diamond Sutra, Chapter III, on The True Principle of Mahayana, 金剛經 , 大乘正宗分第三) which means the ultimate suchness of nirvana.

Another meaning is its use in reference to the death of Buddhas. This is referred to as 入涅槃 , entering into nirvana, where there is neither ending (death) nor arising (birth). To say that there is would still be attached to samsara.

'No-abiding', 無住

無 , no, none; 住 , abiding, staying, dwelling. Thus, 無住 , 'no-abiding' would be not to allow your thoughts to dwell on and thereby to become attached to anything. Particularly to dwell on the past, the present, or the future ties one up in knots.

Glossary A

'No-thought' 無念　無妄念即正念

Actually this means no thoughts that are groundless, baseless, impertinent or erroneous. As the Sixth Patriarch says, 'do not link in the past, dwell in the present, nor to stir up the eighty-four thousand kinds of dust in one's thinking'. All such 'dusty' thoughts should not be present---this is 'no-thought'. The residuum is the pure, the virtuous, the beneficial thoughts.

Observation 觀照

Is to reflect, to perceive or to observe one's thoughts as they arise. The words separately are 觀 , to observe, to scrutinize; and 照 , to shine, to reflect. The combination means to observe and to reflect on one's thoughts as they arise. Not only to know the thoughts but the motivation for such thoughts to arise. It is a method of bringing the subconscious out to the conscious, for in the motivation lies many facets of our own character to which we shut our eyes. If we so scrutinize with prajna, we can uproot many of our erroneous thoughts.

Opposite shore 彼岸

In contrast to the samsara life of a continuous round of births and deaths, which is this shore 此岸 , the opposite shore is beyond the stream of dharma which flows between this shore and the other. It is the attainment of Buddhahood.

Original Mind 本心

The original pristine heart or mind; one's own heart. The innate mind, the one that is inherently pure and quiet.

Perfect view सम्यग्दृष्टि 正見

Samyagdrsti, right views, understanding the four noble truths; the first of the 八正道 ; "knowledge of the four noble truths". In its general use in this sutra, it is the views based on the Patriarch's teachings and those of the Buddha's. It is the virtuous, the truthful views rather than our own conception of what is right. It is the orthodox Dharma.

Precepts, sila शील 戒

Sila are the precepts, the commands, the prohibitions, the disciplines and the rules. The five usually given are: (1) Not to kill; (2) Not to steal; (3) Not to commit adultery; (4) Not to speak falsely; (5) Not to drink excessively. Of course, these refer not only to the

179

Glossary A

deeds but more emphatically to the thoughts. Moreover, in actual practice all malicious, unnecessary and unworthy thoughts should be discarded until the heart and mind is pure. It is only after this that one can practice the deeper concepts.

Repentance - Resolution or Repentance, Ksamayati दमयति 懺悔
Repentance, 懺 ; resolution, 悔 . In the academic sense, 懺 is usually taken as the transliteration of ksama and 悔 as its translation ---thus both means repentance. In colloquial usage the term in its usual combination of 懺悔 carries the meaning of repenting for errors, or regret for one's wrongs. In its specialized usage in Buddhism, which the Sixth Patriarch brings out in Chapter VI, 懺 and 悔 carries distinctive and important meanings of its own. 懺 is both the acknowledgement and the repentance of one's wrongs. Acknowledgement means that a person is fully aware that he is wrong. So we use repentance for 懺 . As to 悔 , in Buddhism, it carries more meaning than just regret. Its emphasis is on a heartfelt resolution never to commit these wrongs again. As the Sixth Patriarch says, unless the latter aspect is completely manifest then one is still 愚迷 , ignorant and deluded. Thus, whenever repentance is used alone, it carries the meaning of repentance and resolution.

Resolution, Ksamayati दमयति 悔
See repentance.

Root, mula मूल 根
根 , mula, root, basis, that which is ingrained, the innate characteristic of a person's nature, e.g. 善根 , would be virtuous roots and 惡根 would be roots of evil in a person's nature. The latter must be thoroughly eradicated on the road to Buddhism.
下根 , shallow roots, poorly endowed, base, low, or devious character. 上根 , superior endowment, keen witted, high character. An extremely interesting aspect of 根 , or thought-patterns is the fact that a person carries into this life the thought-patterns that he has developed in his previous lives, for instance, that of being angry. Because of this, a person frequently may be very angry, yet because of his habituation to it, he would have a very difficult time, first, in understanding it, and secondly, in removing it.

Samadhi, equanimity, imperturbability, meditation समाधि 定
This is not to be construed as being entirely without feelings or emotions and to be immobile in the face of another's distress. Rather,

180

this equanimity has the sense of being in balance regardless of what the turmoil may be. It is the imperturbability of an efficient physician in time of critical emergency. The emotions of mercy and compassion are not absent but they become goads to greater constructive activity rather than to weeping, wailing and caterwauling.

Sambhogakaya सम्भोगकाय 報身
報 , retribution, reward.
身 , body.
Reward body, the sambhoga-kaya of a Buddha, in which he enjoys the reward of his labours. One of three bodies of the Trikaya.
In this sutra, the Patriarch shows that the Sambhogakaya is in our self-nature---that when the genuine nature is not colored by either virtue or vice then it is the perfect Sambhogakaya Buddha. See Chapter VI.

Self-nature, svabhava स्वभाव 自性
In the Chinese, 自 , is self, own, one's own, and 性 , nature, spirit, soul---so that 自性 , is one's innate nature, or one's natural nature. The use of natural here is in the pristine sense of the original state. To arrive at this natural state by the freeing of all bonds of attachments and defilements is one of the important points of this sutra.

Six Gates 六門 , or six organs 六根 , six indriyas.
Literally, 六 , six, 門 , doors, gates, openings. In combination, the words though stating the six entrances or gates, actually means the organs themselves i.e. eye, ear, nose, tongue, body and sense-center.

Six qualities or gunas षड् गुण 六塵
See under gunas

Six senses, vijnanas षड् विज्ञान 六識
The six senses are the six qualitative perceptive functions e.g. seeing, hearing, smelling, tasting, touching and ideation performed by its respective organ in response to stimuli.

Skandhas, five पञ्च स्कन्ध 五蘊
The five aggregates or components or attributes of a person.
1. 色 , rupa, matter, form i.e. the physical form as related to the five sense organs.

181

2. 受 , vedara, sensation, feeling, reception, the functioning of the mind in connection with things.

3. 想 , sanjna, conception, or discerning, the function of the mind in distinguishing.

4. 行 , samskara, the functioning of the mind regarding likes and dislikes, good and evil.

5. 識 , vijnana, mental faculty, and knowledge in regard to cognition and perception, discriminative function in affairs and incidents.

Straightforward 平直

Even, level, tranquil, straightforward, honest, balanced. It refers to a heart and mind that is uncluttered by any evil, unfettered by any attachment.

Suchness, tathata तथता 如
Such, tatha तथा

Literally, so, thus, in such a manner, like, as. In Buddhism it is used as the reality, the suchness of all things---the nature of things as it is. It is used frequently with 真 , genuine, true, (or this word is implied) in combination as 真如 , bhutatathata. In this sense it means the ultimate reality, the absolute which is to be found in the self-nature as---'the true suchness of the self-nature'.

It is also commonly used as 'as is' 如是 , 如是 , 是 meaning is being---so that the words together (imply) ---'as it is, - so it is'. The inference being that we accept all things as they are without distorting them by our own ingrained prejudices and biases.

Suffering, duhkha दुःख 苦

Bitterness; unhappiness, suffering, pain, distress, misery, difficulty. There are lists of two, three, four, five, eight, and ten categories; the two are internal, i.e. physical and mental, and external, i.e. attacks from without; the four are birth, growing old, illness, and death; the eight are these four along with the pain of parting from the loved, of meeting with the hated, of failure in one's aims and that caused by the five skandhas.

Sutra सूत्र 經

Classical works, but more commonly used in Sanskrit to refer to the sermons of the Buddha. In Chinese the usage is broader and includes the works of the sages.

Glossary A

Tao, marga मार्ग 道

Marga, a way, road, the right path, the true principle. The way to liberation through enlightenment. The true inherent nature of the universe.

It is used as the teachings of Lao-Tzu and his followers are the Taoists. The term is also used in Buddhism as the way and, the path, and the Dharma.

Taint, contaminate, discolor 染

Also to dye, to be infected with---used for the defilements, the passions. If one has these anxieties in one's mind, one is contaminated by them 有染 , and thus is still deluded and ignorant 愚迷 .

Ten thousand things 萬法

All things, includes all things with a noumenal or phenomenal existence. Also the means, all methods, as in 'a master should know the ten thousand methods' of teaching.

萬 , ten thousand, is used in the sense of all, complete, so many as to be innumerable.

Three poisons 三毒 , also three evils 三惡

The three poisons are 貪 , greediness or desires; 嗔 , anger, hate, or resentment; and 癡 , stupidity, ignorance, unintelligence and attachment to things or ideas which one is reluctant or unwilling to give up even when one knows they are wrong. These are the root sources of the anxieties, delusions and passions.

Three refuges, trisarana त्रिशरण 三歸依

The three formulas of refuge or vows expressed to the 三寶 the Three Gems, i.e. 佛 to the Buddha; 法 the Dharma; 僧 the Sangha. The formulas are 歸依佛 , Buddham saranam gacchami, I take refuge in the Buddha; 歸依法 , Dharmam saranam gacchami, I take refuge in the Dharma; 歸依僧 , Sangham saranam gacchami, I take refuge in the Brotherhood (monks). Compare this with the Sixth Patriarch's discussion.

Tranquil cessation 寂滅

The state of being unruffled, undisturbed and quietly cheerful. The complete absence of redundancy in the mind. It is cognizance without agitation. This is a practice towards liberation---but it is occasionally mistaken for nirvana itself.

183

Trikaya **त्रिकाय** 三身 or 三寶身
The threefold body or nature of a Buddha, i.e. the Dharmakaya, 法身, Sambhogakaya, 報身, and the Nirmanakaya 化身.
Note in Chapter VI the way the Patriarch places the Trikaya within one's own self.

Vijnana **विज्ञान** 識
The art of distinguishing, or perceiving, or recognizing; discerning, understanding, comprehending; distinction, intelligence, knowledge, science, learning---wisdom. Also see 六識 six senses.

Virtue 德
See merit-virtue.

Void, emptiness, sunya **शून्य** 空
There are several meanings to this term. One is that one empties the mind, so that it is completely silent and thus to think of nothing. This the Sixth Patriarch has said is a deluded, a warped view.
Void as used here, refers to the mind being like the emptiness of space in which all things can be contained, yet there is not a single thing to which one becomes attached. The limitless space represents the breadth of the person's heart and mind in regards to all matters. It refers to the greatness of the tranquility of a person's mind which is never disturbed by any innate or acquired attachment.

Wisdom, prajna **प्रज्ञा** 智慧
Wisdom, understanding and discernment. It is the power to grasp the underlying principle of things. It is frequently used together with 智, jnana, knowledge in the sense of wisdom based upon vast knowledge.

Yana **यान** 乘
A vehicle, any means of conveyance; a term applied to Buddhism as carrying men to liberation. The two chief divisions are 小乘, Hinayana and 大乘, Mahayana, the great vehicle. In the Mahayana, there is the desire to spread the knowledge of liberation for all to follow and the desire to lead all to Buddhahood.
Whereas, in the Hinayana, there is more of the idea of self-liberation. Actually, in the panorama of Buddhism, Hinayana is not a different type of Buddhism, it is perhaps more the groundwork, the basic prerequisite for its more advanced practice in Mahayana.

GLOSSARY B

SANSKRIT OR ENGLISH AND CHINESE

Glossary B

Sanskrit or English and Chinese

1

一乘 Ekayana

3

三毒 three poisons

三身 Trikaya

三惡 also three poisons

三歸依 three refuges

大悟 awakening, great

大乘 yana

4

五蘊 skandha

六門 six gates

六塵 gunas

六識 six senses

天 devas

心 mind

化身 Nirmanakaya

5

四大 four elements

四相 four perspectives

四衆 four classes

四智 four wisdoms

平直 straightforward

末那識 mano-vijnana

正見 perfect view

玄 mystery

生滅 arising and ceasing

本心 original mind

功德 merit-virtue

6

如 suchness

自性 self-nature

邪見 biased views

因果 karma

因緣 causative incidents

7

佛性 Buddha-nature

Note: For further discussion, see corresponding word in Glossary A

Glossary B

坐禅 meditation

戒 precepts

阿賴耶識 Alayavijnana

8

定 samadhi

法身 Dharmakaya

法界 dharmadhatu

法相 formal phenomena

空 void

劫 kalpas

彼岸 opposite shore

9

度 deliverance

染 taint

迷 deluded

苦 suffering

10

悟 awakening

悔 resolution

根 root

乘 yana

11

清淨 clear and quiet

寂滅 tranquil cessation

12

涅槃 nirvana

道 Tao

無住 no-abiding

無念 no-thought

無相 formless

菩提 bodhi

菩薩 Bodhisattva

煩惱 defilements

智 jnana

智慧 wisdom

報身 Sambbogakaya

萬法 ten thousand things

Glossary B

13			**24**	
經	sutra		觀照 observation	
福	fortune			
福田	field of merit			
障	encumbrances			
意	intellect			

14

塵 gunas

15

德 merit-virtue

摩訶般若波羅密多 Mahaprajnaparamita

16

緣 incident

19

識 vijnana

20

懺悔 repentance

189